D0592098

When
TROUBLE
Comes

When
TROUBLE
Comes

A Christian View of Evil, Sin, and Suffering

James E. Sellers

ABINGDON PRESS
new york • nashville

WHEN TROUBLE COMES

Copyright © *MCMLX by Abingdon Press*

Library of Congress Catalog Card Number: 60-5476

SET UP, PRINTED, AND BOUND BY THE
PARTHENON PRESS, AT NASHVILLE,
TENNESSEE, UNITED STATES OF AMERICA

TO

M. A. West

AND

Graceville

Preface

NEARLY EVERYONE WOULD AGREE THAT LIFE INCLUDES BUILT-in hardships; you can't live without suffering. It has always been that way. Riches, an optimistic frame of mind, good fortune—these advantages may make life easier in some ways, but they won't do away with hardship and suffering. Part of the risk of being alive is to take your chances with unpleasant chapters of existence, and, some would say, your willingness to take such risks is an index to the degree you're really alive.

Of course, life is not all suffering and danger. And even a life filled with hardship can be a life of happiness. Yet it has never been easy for men and women struck by misfortune to understand how or why it could have happened to *them*. Just as predictable as our fate of undergoing hardship is our curiosity about *why* we must do so—and that explains this book.

In a way, the least satisfactory approach to the hardships of life is to read or talk about them. If I have a toothache, I don't want it explained so much as I want it stopped. And perhaps even more than either one of these—explanation or healing—what I need is the courage to face and go through with the suffering while it lasts. So it's certain we can't learn much about suffering on the basis of speculation or study alone. Suffering is a necessary and mysterious part of life, and all the talk in the world won't change that.

At the same time mature people wish to think and reflect on the important things in their lives. Suffering has to be thought about and talked about precisely because it is so deeply central to life. Suffering is a problem (or better, a *mystery*) that has captured men's minds throughout history.

The writers of the Old Testament wrestle mightily with the question. One whole book—Job—is devoted to this single matter. So are many of the Psalms. Theologians and philosophers from the fourth century's Augustine to the twentieth century's John Dewey have grappled with it. Like these men, the sincere Christian will want to consider the question of suffering—even if he knows in advance he can't answer the question by thought alone.

To make some progress we can start with several assumptions. One is that suffering and evil are somehow tied up together. Another is that suffering at its worst is a *spiritual* problem more than a *physical* one. A heartache, generally speaking, causes deeper suffering than a toothache.

A third assumption is that you have to apply the question personally. You won't really get much personal light on your own suffering if you study it solely as a problem of nerve structure—or as a problem of abstract philosophy. Rather you must ask: "What is my life all about? Why do I have to take these risks? And why is my fortune so bad so much of the time?" Indeed, you must not only ask: "Why do *I* suffer?" but also: "Why do I cause *others* to suffer?"

Finally, you must assume that you are *not* going to find out all the answers. You must be open and honest in your thinking and your reading. You must be willing to talk about the problem without feeling sorry for yourself. Above all, you must be willing to listen to God and to admit that here you may be face to face with a mystery.

JAMES E. SELLERS

Contents

Part II: SIN

Part III: SUFFERING

PART I

PHYSICAL EVIL

I

Evil Is a Part of Things

THE PLACE TO BEGIN, PERHAPS, IS WITH EVIL ITSELF. OUR chief interest may lie, to be sure, in the painful results of evil, especially within human life. These results we usually discuss under the heading of suffering. Yet we can hardly look into the outcome without first getting clear on the meaning of evil itself.

Undoubtedly we would be much better off if we had two words in English for evil. The Germans do have: *Übel* and *Böse*. The first refers to *physical* evil—storms, floods, death, and other natural occurrences that bring destruction and pain into life. The second refers to *moral* evil—sin of all kinds, from personal acts of wrongdoing to spectacular group transgressions like war.

We can feel something of this same distinction when we compare two English words like "kill" and "murder." The former can be used to describe the taking of life by accidental or natural means. *Murder,* however, always carries a heavy moral element as part of its meaning; a murder is always a kind of sin-ridden evil rather than a blameless natural evil; it is always somebody's fault.

Both kinds of evil cause suffering, of course, and in most practical situations we find them mingled beyond separation. The murderer, for example, must use physical or natural methods to carry out his crime. Just the same, we shall find it helpful to talk about evil by breaking down our subject into the two kinds—natural evil and moral evil.

Our first step is to look at *Übel*—the physical or natural kind of evil, beginning with a case study. Then, in later pages, we can go into *Böse,* the second kind—moral evil or sin. After that we will be ready to come back to the main question: Why is life so hard? Or as the author of Job conceived the question: Why do the innocent suffer?

The Day the Wind Blew

It is not easy to understand why, on September 16, 1928, so much trouble and calamity should have been heaped on the people of South Florida.

When that day started, the universe seemed a pretty well-run place—especially to the residents of the resort areas and truck-farming sections in the vast "fingertip" of Florida below Lake Okeechobee.

Only two years before a big and bruising hurricane had swept through, but by now most everyone had forgotten about it. Hotels in Miami and Miami Beach had patched up their torn roofs and other damage from the last storm.

Highway construction crews had built back washed-out roads, which were now in heavier use than ever. Tourists and land buyers were flocking south.

Not far from Miami, in the farm region south of Lake Okeechobee, growers tackled a big harvest. They had finally learned how to claim the rich soil around the lake, turn it from a wilderness into a garden. Black and fertile, the low approaches to the lake produced astounding crops.

Harvests were usually so abundant the local residents couldn't handle them alone. Farm laborers came from Georgia and other places to the north, glad of the chance to work a few weeks. This year such laborers were needed by the thousands, and they lived in temporary quarters on the farms and plantations around the big lake.

Few of these men and women, busy with their chores, spent much time worrying about the dangers from weather which could be expected at this time of year. It was common knowledge that the water level in the lake was considerably higher than some of the farmlands around the lake, but then the land was protected by a stout levee that held the water back.

Three days earlier a hurricane had hit the island of Puerto Rico off Florida's east coast. No one, not even the weather bureau, figured it would veer westward enough to hit Florida. Then it changed course. On September 16 the hurricane plowed into Palm Beach, heading northwest.

At Lake Okeechobee the hurricane produced a northwest wind which blew stronger and stronger across the water. Finally, the same thing happened to the lake that

19

happens to a teaspoonful of coffee if you blow on it too hard.

The water in Lake Okeechobee piled up in the southeast corner. Soon it spilled violently over the levee and broke upon the land in monstrous waves, pounded with piledriver force by the hurricane wind.

A mountain of water rushed over the plantations, dashing houses and buildings. Frightened residents went upstairs—if they were lucky enough to live in two-story houses. Some families crept into their attics; then, as the water continued to rise, they forced holes through their roofs and climbed on top.

In that wind-driven flood of 1928 untold hundreds of people drowned. No one has ever made an accurate count. There was no way of telling how many scores of migrant farm laborers were swept away. Estimates of the toll in human lives ranged from 1,000 to 2,500. Whole families and even villages disappeared, wiped out by the wall of water. Every single resident of the community of Pelican Bay was lost. It is safe to guess that not less than 1,250 permanent and temporary residents of South Florida died in the terrible hurricane of 1928.

What Does It All Mean?

This tragic hurricane clearly illustrates what we mean by *natural evil*. Why call it natural? Because storms and floods are part of nature. In the Bible we are reminded over and over that God *made* creation that way. Here is a typical affirmation from the psalmist:

He it is who makes the clouds rise at the end of the earth,
  who makes lightnings for the rain
  and brings forth the wind from his storehouses.
                                                    —*Ps. 135:7*

And why call it *evil?* Because such catastrophes result
in human suffering. Meteorologists suspect that hurricanes
have been sweeping across the West Indies and Florida for
thousands of years. The 1928 blow and its accompanying
flood were nothing new. We think of it as something evil
because it became a part of human history—it invaded
human affairs and brought destruction, injury, and death.
A hurricane takes lives, tears up property, forces men to
change their plans, postpone their projects, pour their
energy and wealth into repair work.

But how can a creation of God's be evil? Why should
God have created a universe in which there are natural
catastrophes—famines, floods, earthquakes, sickness, epidemics, and death? These are questions we shall not be
able to answer adequately, at least not in one chapter.
Nevertheless, we can get some help by looking at the
question of natural evil from the Bible's point of view.

The prophet Isaiah insists that faith in God means we
must see God as the creator of all things, even those things
which upset human plans, pride, and property. According
to Isaiah, God declares:

I form light and create darkness,
  I make weal and create woe,
  I am the Lord, who do all these things.
                                                    —*Isa. 45:7*

21

The prophet Amos says something very similar. "Does evil befall a city," he asks, "unless the Lord has done it?" (Amos 3:6.) Whatever we have is from God. He both blesses us and sends us trials. God is not great unless he is Lord of all creation, and our faith in him is not large unless we admit it.

Is God Cruel?

Yet we must say more. We cannot leave it at that. The God known to Christians is a loving God. We do not believe God created storms and floods and other "natural evils" because he wants to see suffering.

Look at it another way: God is *mighty*, but not *cruel*. At least that is the conclusion to which the writer of Psalm 147 comes. On the one hand, this song declares: "Great is our Lord, and abundant in power." On the other hand, this might God uses for man's benefit, though man may not always be able to understand just how. Our knowledge that the Lord is great is the best possible reason for resting in him and praising him. Though he scatters frost like ashes and snow like wool,

> He heals the brokenhearted,
> and binds up their wounds.
>
> . . . .
>
> he prepares rain for the earth,
> he makes grass grow upon the hills.
>
> —*Ps. 147:8*

The Christian must go one step further, we can say

22

now, and declare positively that God's creation is *good*—catastrophes and all.

To be "good" creation does not have to be devoid of trials and tests and hardships. It is good because it fits man for fellowship with God. In a way, then, creation is good precisely because it *does* test us. Think of what life would be like if there were no difficulties, no setbacks, no disappointments. Without danger and want (which is the same as saying without *natural evil*) there would be no human progress, no civilization. In short, men would not have advanced beyond savages, and they would hardly therefore have *used* the life God has given them.

Think for a moment of the Hebrews in Old Testament days. If Abraham's descendants had not *suffered* as slaves in Egypt, they probably would not have wanted to make the Exodus to the Promised Land. Furthermore, if their wanderings in the wilderness hadn't been so severe, they might have been content to remain as nomads, instead of forging on to the new land, where their unique religious heritage took flower.

Or take Americans and their land. If nature presented us no problems—no floods to control, no cold to fight off, no hunger pangs, no distances to conquer—there would be no science of engineering, no modern farming methods, no industry, *no America*. God's creation is "good" for us only if it makes us into better men, physically and spiritually, and it could not make us into better men if it did not make us work, and think, and sweat, and feel pain—and even threaten us with death.

When God chooses followers, he never offers them a

life free of hardships and problems. He invited the Hebrews to follow Moses out of Egypt, but they could not accept this invitation without venturing forth and, therefore, without letting themselves in for rough going. In the trackless wilds of the Near East they were often hungry, often thirsty, often tired, often in despair. They did not become fully God's followers until they were willing to accept such risks—for following God means putting all else aside and facing the dangers.

Evil is real. There is no getting around it.

What God asks of us is that we trust him. We can be sure we will run into natural evil and suffering. That is part of life. Somehow, though, faith assures us these trials are no more than we should expect. Neither the prospect of hunger or poverty, nor the threat of death should throw us into despair. The terrors of existence can be matched by faith in God's purpose—as Moses convinced the Hebrews, and Jesus assured the fear-stricken disciples once when waves and water nearly swamped their boat (Matt. 8:26) .

For the follower of Christ life on this earth, despite its dangers, is *good*. This does not mean there is no natural evil and no suffering. It does mean that life can be rewarding to faith even in the midst of these difficulties.

Profit from Tragedy

Let's go back to the 1928 Florida hurricane a moment. All over America people offered clothes, food, and money to the homeless survivors. If the tragedy made men a little more interested in each other, that alone means it had its helpful outcome.

But, in addition, the catastrophe led to renewed effort by men of courage to overcome hurricanes.

Spurred on by the 1928 hurricane's victory over men, Americans of the following generation developed new ways of weather prediction and communication. Nowadays, through radar, scouting planes, and radio, we can usually stay one jump ahead of tropical storms. We can hope to avoid the mass tragedy that came with the wind in 1928. Building on a defeat, civilization inched ahead, and those who cared to look for God found him, a source of courage and energy amid life's blows.

Let us not be too easily put at ease, however. If we have conquered hurricanes, we have hardly conquered natural evil. It is like the hydra: cut off one head, and two grow back in its place. By subduing a particular form of evil, such as the hurricane, we haven't eliminated suffering or death. The only real, lasting victory over nature is one achieved within the human spirit when we can break through our troubles to make a venturous affirmation of faith.

Our main discovery in this first chapter has been: *Evil is a part of things.* So is suffering. God is not "cruel" or "terrible" for our Christian faith tells us his purposes, even when they involve natural evil, are good and meant for our benefit in the long run. We find "evil" at large in the world of nature because men realize themselves and use their gifts only when they have to deal with hardship, suffering, and death. And we know that commitment to God's way asks us to face all such dangers with courage.

WHAT DO YOU THINK?

1. Why should God have created a universe in which there are natural catastrophes—famines, floods, earthquakes, sickness, epidemics, death?

2. Do you think scientific and technical progress will ever eliminate disease? Physical suffering? Death?

3. Augustine remarked that nothing is entirely evil if it is a part of God's creation. Do you agree?

4. The Selective Service system has found a distressing proportion of American youth physically unfit. Could one reason be the lack of sufficient "natural evil"—hardships, trials—in the lives of Americans?

5. Does everyone profit from tragedy?

6. It is a custom in legal proceedings to call natural disasters "acts of God." How would you explain this term to an ignorant savage whose tribe had drowned in a flood?

7. Could an avalanche that killed or injured no one be described as evil? What if it killed only animals? What if it destroyed timber or other natural resources that would have eventually been useful to human beings?

II

How to Explain Hard Luck

DANIEL DOUGH, JR., NINETEEN, COPY BOY FOR THE NORFOLK *Virginian-Pilot,* happened to have sandy, brown, close-cropped hair parted to the left. With it went hazel eyes and a rather full face. Judged by standards of looks he was fortunate enough to have a clean-cut, healthy appearance well above the average.

Judged by circumstances, though, Daniel Dough's looks came close to representing a curse upon him, rather than a gift from nature, for a Norfolk bank teller identified Dough as the man who had entered the bank and tried to hold it up.

If all had been left up to "nature," Daniel Dough, Jr., might well have gone to jail for a crime he didn't commit.

Fortunately the real would-be robber, one James Anderson, read in the papers that the FBI had picked up Dough. Conscience-stricken, Anderson surrendered.

Dough and Anderson were an amazing pair of "lookalikes." Only when they were taken together to the bank could the teller correctly identify Anderson as the man who had attempted the holdup.

In cases like this we are struck by nature's mysterious ways. When he was taken in hand by the FBI simply because of the way he happened to look, Daniel Dough was the victim of a mild form of "natural evil." He was born with what very nearly became a menace to his freedom: sandy hair, hazel eyes, a full face.

Can We "Blueprint" Evil?

Why should it have happened at all? And why, in particular, should this streak of tough luck have happened to Daniel Dough, Jr., of Norfolk?

Or take the case of a high-school girl who went to the Florida beaches for a month's vacation.

"Fifteen minutes in that sun," she said later, "and I was all red and blistered. I was with some other girls, and they all came home with nice suntans. What's wrong with me? Why couldn't I get a tan like other people?"

Here, too, is another mild affliction at the hands of "natural evil"—perhaps a major affliction in the mind of a sixteen-year-old girl. Why couldn't everyone be born with skin that will resist sunburn? Why did this girl have to be singled out for the somewhat unhappy fate of not being able to get a tan?

To move the question into more serious territory, we can ask why some children are born with crossed eyes and crippled limbs. Or we can ask why the family of seven down the street lost their father so tragically, or why a gifted piano player was so unfortunate as to shatter his elbow in a fall. Why, in short, does nature seem to deal us blows so unreasonably and unpredictably? If we could just figure out why, we sometimes think, bearing our hard lot would be much easier.

We have already reached the conclusion that natural evil is part of the scene. It is here whether we like it or not; the Christian accepts it, in some way, as part of God's creation. But the fact that evil must be accepted only increases our desire to have a "blueprint" of it. The more we are confronted with evil, the harder we press to learn nature's innermost secrets. Our inquiry in this chapter will take us through some of the many explanations of natural evil that Christians have proposed.

Five Points of View

Even when men resolve to stick to the Bible, they still come to all sorts of different conclusions about what the Bible says. Though most, if not all, of the explanations of evil common to Americans are amply fortified by biblical references, they vary considerably among themselves. A number of these attempts to explain evil have become well-known and much-used in our own day. Our job is to look at some of the most formidable ones now in vogue. Then we may go further and try to decide for ourselves what to say when someone asks: "Why do Christians believe in the reality of evil? What can you say about the way evil works?"

1. *Evil is just in your mind.* If a fact is troublesome enough, one natural way of explaining it is to pretend it really isn't there. This is an ancient solution which has not

diminished in popularity with the ages. It appears in an interesting modern form in America.

Professional journalists have great respect for the *Christian Science Monitor,* a daily newspaper published at Boston, Massachusetts. This fine paper has won many awards for its reporting, its keen analysis of the news, and its clean typography.

Even so, this newspaper has what seems to many an odd practice. The editors of the *Monitor* do not like to talk about *death*—or many other kinds of natural evil. Its reporters will avoid, if possible, making use of the word. They usually write that a person has "passed on," where the same account in any other paper would probably say the person has "died."

Besides, the *Monitor* generally stays away from news about crime and catastrophe. If it does use such stories, it plays down the sensational and shocking elements. Its restraint on such subjects is very likely one of the reasons the *Monitor* has won a reputation for sane, decent journalism. Nevertheless, not all Christians can readily accept the theological reasoning which lies behind the *Monitor's* reluctance to broach the subject of death and other unpleasant aspects of existence.

The *Monitor* is owned and operated by the Church of Christ, Scientist. The Christian Scientists, following the teachings of their founder, the late Mary Baker Eddy, take the fundamental view that *evil is not real.* Such experiences as suffering, sorrow, sickness, death, and sin, they say, are "mistakes"—errors in our minds.

Men run into all these troubles because their beliefs are

wrong. If they would think the right things, have faith in the manner Mrs. Eddy urged, say the Christian Scientists, their ills could be healed. Their errors leading them into evil would be done away with.

Most of us have run into at least one person who can tell how an illness has been cured through faith healing or holding the proper beliefs. Apparently, there is no limit to the expectations of devoted members of the sect. Some Christian Scientists are even sure their tooth decay has been healed through right thinking.

Mrs. Eddy and her followers quote the Bible at length to prove their views. They like especially to talk about Jesus' work of healing—as when he cured a man with paralysis because the man and his friends had great faith (Mark 2:3-12).

What should we think of Christian Science? Well, all Christians should believe in the healing power of faith. The story about the paralytic could mean no less than that faith in God benefits our whole person. To the men of Jesus' day, health of "body" and health of "soul" were more or less one and the same thing. Faith in God and love of others, Jesus seemed to be saying, is the best possible treatment for your mind, spirit, and body. And we can today believe no less than that.

But to believe in the healing power of faith does not require us to believe that disease and evil are unreal. Faith should never be thought of simply as a quick way of avoiding life's hardships.

There is always the probability that God will *require* us to do a certain amount of suffering. We may be asked to suffer with our bodies as well as our hearts and minds. And here faith comes to the rescue not by persuading us that evil is unreal, but rather by offering us courage to bear our burdens.

2. *Evil is real, but not God's.* Another common way of explaining evil is to admit it is real but deny that God has anything to do with it. Both Christians and non-Christians have shown a fancy for this line of thought.

Among Christians, the usual approach is to build up Satan into a permanent, evil force opposite God in the universe; then anything that is unpleasant, or wrong, or disorderly, or upsetting in the creation can be attributed to Satan. God is thus left with clean hands; he does not have to be involved in the production of evil. Since Satan is taken to be independent of God, we don't have to say that God is the cause of evil and suffering.

Again, it is easy to quote the Bible to prove this point of view. It's true, we find very little about the devil in the Old Testament—"Satan" as a proper name for the devil, in fact, appears only a few times, most notably in the opening scenes of Job. But Satan and his devils are very much in evidence through the New Testament. By reading these passages a certain way, you can make the demons look like independent agents, standing against God instead of falling under his control.

Take the story of the raving maniacs in Matthew—the episode about two men with "demons" in them. When Jesus saw these madmen, he took pity on them right away. He ordered the demons to go away and leave the men alone. The demons promptly transferred their activities to a nearby herd of swine, and the swine rushed headlong into the sea. (Matt. 8:28-34.)

Notice closely what happens here. According to the story in Matthew, the men were said to be mad or ill because of the demons which lived in them. Jesus comes on the scene and restores the men to wholeness by driving away the demons.

But the demons seem to be the immortal agents of an enemy god, not one as powerful as God himself, perhaps, but at least powerful enough to send his agents fearlessly about on earth doing their dirty work. Even when Jesus confronts the demons directly, they do not lie down and die. They simply shift their operations to another place —the pigs. In any case, the demons might be supposed to be only small fry—mere jackstraws of the real Evil One, who remains at large.

From such an interpretation as this we might get the impression that God has only a limited and partial power over the forces of evil. He is not to be charged in any way with responsibility for the things that go wrong among men.

A neat theory, this. It has a major flaw, however. It pictures God as being in control of something less than all of creation. So long as Satan and his demons are free to do more or less as they please, then God must turn out to be limited in his might and power.

If we examine the Bible's references to Satan carefully, we find an entirely different picture. Satan, from the Bible's point of view, is so far from being independent of God that the author of Job actually portrays him as one of God's own agents!

In the prologue of Job Satan is ranked with the "sons of God" (Job 1:6). His special function appears to be to test men, to try their faith severely by bringing woe and temptations upon them. But always, Satan is under God's control; he must seek permission to subject Job to torment, and God forces him, without getting too much of an argument, to promise not to take Job's life. (Job 1:12).

Among many moderns Satan has had rough going. Science, book learning, and laboratory findings seemingly have almost done away with the devil. It is difficult, to say the least, for an educated person to believe nowadays in a real Satan, complete with hoofs, horns, and pitchfork.

Yet many of those who discount Satan as a personality share completely in the theory of evil we have just been describing. To them, whatever evil forces are at work in the world are independent of God. These forces may be called "environment" by some, or they may be called "property" or "wealth" by the Communists. But the point is the same: the source of evil is seen as something operating independently in the universe. Scientists, socialists, and Communists are interested in the argument for their own varied purposes, of course; few take up the subject in order to defend God's goodness, as Christians usually are doing when they attempt to make the devil all-powerful. Yet the end result of all these theories discounting God's part in evil is the same: they rob God of stature and might and reduce him to a limited God. Among such faiths as Communism, God is reduced to nothing at all.

What should Christians believe about the devil? That is up to the individual, of course, to a very large degree. But the writers of the Old and New Testaments are practically unanimous on one point: whatever our conception of Satan may be, there is no eternal force of evil—devil or otherwise—that is *independent* of God. If there is a devil, he is somehow God's, and if his actions go contrary to God's will, he will have to submit in the long run. Even if there is no literal devil and evil resides in an impersonal "environment," it, too, is ultimately under the control of God's hand.

3. *Evil is only temporary.* Much more popular than belief in Satan among Americans is belief in the "happy ending." Not that there is anything unchristian about happy endings, but there is scant support for the view that the happy ending to life is just around the corner, and that all evil can soon be cleaned up by men and their inventions.

Today, we know that penicillin, a remarkable drug made from ordinary mold, is quite limited in its powers. But when it was introduced in the early 1940's, certain journalists and medical men (who should have known better) hailed it as virtually the answer to man's health problems. Here are titles of some of the articles which appeared in our magazines: "Cannibal Mold More Powerful Germ-Killer Than Sulfa Drugs." "Miracle Drug." "New Bacteria Compound, More Potent Than Sulfa Drugs, Is Produced by a Common Bread Mold," "Saved by Penicillin."

Before long, however, doctors noticed a discouraging development. Penicillin sometimes seemed to lose its punch. With certain diseases it came to be less and less effective. Research eventually showed that some strains of bacteria were able to develop an immunity to the mold. Some germs even learned, apparently, to thrive on penicillin!

Even more discouraging, entirely new diseases occasionally appeared, completely resistant to attack by penicillin.

From all medical science can learn, diseases are an inescapable part of the environment. They are not temporary, and they are not going to disappear, even with the best drugs and care medicine can provide.

Just as we like to dream that disease is only temporary and can soon be wiped out, we try to make the same assumption about all kinds of natural evil. But, if we may take the New Testament seriously, reality seems to point in the other direction. Men will always be subject to the changes and chances of nature. Christ offers us courage and rest, but he does not *guarantee* us even a roof over our head (Matt. 8:20). We must find our peace not in inventions and scientific advantages, as useful as these are; we must rather find it in the midst of risk and danger.

Christian faith, as we have said, sees truth in the belief that life has a happy ending. But the happy ending isn't automatically guaranteed to come tomorrow, or the next day, or the next. The New Testament seems to say that as long as men are men and history is history, men must "take their lumps." Some day, for each of us, there will be some kind of great final chapter, and those who have sought fellowship with God will surely find the "happy ending" that so many have vainly sought (Matt. 8:11). But there is no short cut we can take to avoid life.

4. *Evil is a matter of chance.* Imagine that the copy boy who got mixed up with the bank robber had lived in ancient Greece. If he had indeed gone to jail for a crime he did not commit, here are some of the explanations his friends might have made to him for his bad luck:

"Fate has sent you this misfortune."

"God doesn't care what happens to you one way or the other."

"God wouldn't deliberately send evil on us, but on the other hand, he wouldn't lift a finger to keep it off or stoop to help you in any way. After all, you are just an insignificant speck of humanity. Your fate could be of no concern to God."

Not all the Greeks, of course, were doubters and skeptics. The great philosophers, and Plato in particular, spent a great deal of time and effort opposing this way of thought. Yet the skeptical point of view was very popular in the Greek world just before the time of Christ.

A little of this skepticism, in fact, found its way into one book of the Old Testament, Ecclesiastes.

The author of this book more than once falls into a cynical, doubting mood. He appears to believe in these moods that God is really not concerned with the affairs of men. Misfortunes just seem to happen. Life is weary and vain, a repetitious cycle, says this author, "all is vanity" (Eccl. 1:2). Men cannot even find out what is good for them in their few days of life, which pass like a shadow.

Fortunately, this pessimistic mood does not prevail in

37

the Bible. It does not even get too far in the book of Ecclesiastes. For its author elsewhere affirms his confidence in God's purpose.

Skepticism is quite typical of our own day, too. Many people say they believe in God, but they want to make him into something unimportant by their willingness to blame everything on "chance." You can recognize this view easily by the "slogans" used among its holders, such as: "That's the way things are." "That's the way the ball bounces." "That's the way the cooky crumbles."

A pipe fitter at a shipyard once listened to a clergyman explain how every vocation ought to be filled with purpose and interest right down to the last minute of the day. When the clergyman had finished, the pipe fitter objected:

"My job is to make templates—you know, patterns—that show the bends in a piece of pipe. The pipe benders take my templates and make the pipe curve the same way. Then the pipe will fit into the space on the ship it's designed for.

"Making one template is about like making another. I spend the whole day putting little curves into a piece of wire. It gets tiresome. Anyway, I'll never get onto the ship and see the pipes in use. I just can't buy the argument that a job should have an interesting purpose."

There are good answers to the pipe fitter's boredom, but that is not our point right now. What we are interested in seeing is that the character of many jobs in this day and time leads straight to the kind of blind acceptance of fate that sees no purpose in life. Under this view, evil as well as good is likely to be thought of as "just happening,"

38

rather than as taking place in a world where God's purposes are built into everything. That is why the laws of chance may seem more real than anything else.

Christians believe in the laws of chance, but somehow, they also believe in the ultimate control of our destiny by God. Let us be frank and admit that the Church hasn't always found a way to convince men like the skeptical pipe fitter of God's purpose. But we have at least made a start when we recognize the pipe fitter's problem. The Christian gospel was an answer to the skepticism and resignation of the Greek world; it can be an answer to the pipe fitter's boredom of our own.

5. *Evil is part of God's way.* So far, we have considered four views of natural evil—that it is unreal; that it is real but not controlled by God; that it is only temporary and can soon be cleaned up by men; that it is purely an aimless occurrence, the result of the laws of chance or blind fate. Now we can consider one more theory: that evil is real, that it is part of God's creation, and that it exists as one of God's ways of dealing with men.

God never wishes natural evil on us in cruel repayment for sins. That would make God into a narrow-minded moral bookkeeper instead of a God of love and mercy and forgiveness. Some writers of the Old Testament seem to misunderstand God's way here, when they claim that floods, catastrophe, death, military defeat, and so on, are God's punishment for the sins of the Hebrews (see, for example, Judg. 6:1).

We know, from other writers in the Old Testament as well as from nearly all of the New Testament, that God

39

accepts us. He loves us in spite of the sins we commit. All he asks is that we turn to him in trust and repentance. Because he is a great God, he will deal with us largely—not being guided by our past "evil ways" or our "corrupt doings" but offering us his name (Ezek. 20:44).

But love and risk go hand in hand. We have the *chance* to become men because God cares about us; we have the *actual means* of doing so only by accepting, through Christ, the call to put ourselves last, the call to risk everything we possess, including our lives, for the most valuable thing of all: *new life in Christ.*

Natural evil is a permanent part of creation. It comes to all, saint and sinner alike, and like everything else in creation, it is the work of God. Sickness, accidents of birth, catastrophes, and death—these are all part of the venture God asks us to take in peopling his world and serving him.

Augustine struggled for years with the question of evil. How could it come from God? He finally decided that good and evil go together, and that even the most evil things of all have promise for good: "For the Omnipotent God, whom even the heathen acknowledge as the Supreme Power over all, would not allow any evil in his works, unless in his omnipotence and goodness, as the Supreme Good, he is able to bring forth good out of evil." With this statement we have arrived at the main Christian teaching on natural evil, which is called the "doctrine of Providence." In the next chapter we will consider God's Providence at greater length.

WHAT DO YOU THINK?

1. In a tough-minded criticism of Christian notions about God, the Scottish philosopher David Hume advanced the following argument: "Is he [God] willing to prevent evil, but not able? then is he impotent. Is he able, but not willing? then is he malevolent." How would you answer?

2. What is the commonest explanation of evil among Americans? Among your own friends? What is yours?

3. Why have scientific-minded people generally laid aside such concepts as God and Satan in explaining natural events?

4. Consider each of the five explanations of evil outlined above. What, from your point of view, is the main objection to each? What, on the other hand, is the strong point of each?

5. During World War II, at least one Japanese battle fleet was turned back by ocean storms. Does this mean God was opposing the Japanese? How do you explain the destruction of three U. S. destroyers by a typhoon in the same war?

6. Does the notion of happiness rule out the possibility of suffering?

7. The National Safety Council can often predict with only a small error the number of automobile passengers who will die in accidents over a holiday period. How can such predictions be made so accurately? Doesn't this ability prove that the laws of chance are the supreme reality?

III

Does Faith Banish Evil?

HER FACE ETCHED WITH PAIN, MARIE COVINGTON WEST stood in her white dress against the Tennessee August night. Before her, watching intently from benches on the grass, were fellow worshipers, including several children. Writhing in her hands was a deadly rattlesnake—which two minutes before had sunk its fangs into her right arm.

Nine hours later, Mrs. West died. She had refused medical assistance. Her brother, Mansel Covington, under arrest for violating a state law forbidding the careless handling of deadly snakes, attributed her death to her "failing faith in the Lord."

Few Christians would care to interpret the protective function of faith in the same manner that Mrs. West or Mansel Covington did, despite their claim to scriptural authority (Mark 16:18). Rather, most of us would expect an angry rattlesnake held in our hands to bite us, no matter how devout we might be. But the snake has always been the supreme symbol of evil, and the pathetic snake-handling rites held that hot night near Savannah, Tennessee, symbolize a fugitive hope that has crossed the mind of many a Christian. Can faith be an automatic method of banishing evil? If it can, then how?

The Boll Weevil Tragedy

Cotton growers in the United States didn't have to fight the boll weevil until as late as 1892. In this year the snout-nosed, little boring insect crossed the Rio Grande River from Mexico and settled in Texas. Only thirty years later it had multiplied beyond human imagination and infested cotton fields all over the Southwest and South.

Choosy about both its living quarters and its diet, the boll weevil refused to attack any crop except cotton. A lot of good this choosiness was, though! Large sections of the South had depended for years on that one crop. In Mississippi, Alabama, Georgia, among other states, cotton was king.

For these one-crop sections of the South the coming of the boll weevil was a great tragedy—*or was it?*

Ride through southern Alabama today and you will see acres of green pastures. On the pastures you will see beef cattle and dairy herds. You will also find the farmers raising hogs, poultry, and a variety of field crops.

Thanks to the weevil, cotton is no longer king. The farmers who turned from cotton to livestock raising and dairying are better off than they were in the cotton-growing days.

In one southern Alabama community citizens actually

built a monument to the boll weevil. The "tragedy" of the weevil forced them to get out of a one-crop economy there, and now the people see it was the best thing that could have happened to them. Ramshackle, unpainted houses with open "dog-runs" in the middle have been replaced by white-painted, fence-surrounded ranch houses. The horse-drawn plow is gone, and the tractor has taken its place. Instead of living for nine months in the year on salt meat and cornbread, farm families enjoy about as high a standard of eating as other Americans—and a higher one in June and July when home-grown tomatoes, field peas, corn on the cob, and snap beans come in.

We would stretch things to say all this change is to be laid directly to the invasion of the boll weevil, but, beyond the shadow of a doubt, the havoc wrought by this insect two generations ago was a most important factor behind the switchover in farming methods.

Was It "for the Best"?

The boll weevil "tragedy" helps us to see natural evil in the best light: as God's work, in some sense of the word, as a force for good, despite the suffering and pain it causes —and despite our frequent inability to see ahead far enough to sight the good.

By "natural evil" we mean the suffering which men undergo at the hands of nature. As examples of "natural evil" we can include all kinds of catastrophes like floods, earthquakes, fires, and storms. Other instances of "natural evil" include disease, epidemic, sickness, accidents, crop failure, plagues, and dozens of other "acts of nature." We know natural evil in its most powerful form, of course, as *death*.

At this point, we can summarize our progress so far:

1. Natural evil is *real*. It is a part of God's creation and not to be denied.

2. Therefore we cannot explain it as simply *imaginary*, or as caused by some force *outside* of God, or as the workings of blind *chance*.

3. But if evil is *God's work somehow*, we have to be careful not to misunderstand. Natural evil, we know, is not God's revenge against us for our sins—for our God is a great, good God who loves us despite our sins. Christians have found the most satisfactory explanation of natural evil comes out of an attempt to understand God's *Providence*.

Providence comes from the same Latin word as *provide*. If we believe in God's Providence, we believe he somehow *provides* for us. Originally to "provide" meant to "look ahead." Nowadays, however, we usually put some kind of bacon-and-eggs meaning on the word, thinking that "provide" means to "fill up the pantry" or "keep us in groceries."

If we believe in Providence, we believe God will provide, *look ahead* for us. That is, we believe he will take care of us, act in our interest, do what is best. It does *not* mean we will always have plenty of bacon and eggs in the refrigerator, because sometimes the thing we need most is to have to stumble through a few hardships.

Let's go back to the boll weevils for a moment. Most persons who believe in God's Providence would say it was

45

at work in the invasion of the boll weevils. That was doubt-less hard—or impossible—to see at the time the weevils were chewing away. Farmers who were losing their crops suffered both financially and spiritually. Numbers of them went broke. In the long run everyone seems to agree that the coming of the weevils worked out for the best.

In general, that is what we mean to say when we have faith in God's Providence. We mean to say we trust God. It may go hard with us as a result, but we trust God and know that in the end he has the best ideas about what needs to be done.

We can now see that the worst enemy of Providence is our own human, short-sighted way of looking at things. We are so wrapped up in our plans of the moment, we can't look ahead, but that is all the more reason to trust God and call on him in prayer.

Does faith in Providence mean men do nothing for themselves? Of course not. The farmers in South Alabama didn't sit back on their front porches with their hands in their pockets. When the boll weevil took their cotton away, they started experimenting with cows and pasture grasses.

One day somebody discovered that white Dutch clover would grow in the season when regular summer grass was dead. Result: year-round pastures and the promise of a whole new kind of agriculture in the South, built around livestock—beef cattle and dairy herds.

God gave these farmers their chance and even gave them their cows and white Dutch clover—but they had to re-spond for themselves with courage and conviction. Most of all they had to have new hope to replace the hopes lost.

Gustave Aulén, a Swedish bishop, who has thought long and hard about the subject of Providence, comes to three conclusions:

1. God cares for all things.
2. He wills something in everything that happens.
3. The man of faith may confidently place everything in God's hands.

These are convictions that you find sticking out all through the Scripture. In fact, Aulén freely admits he got the idea from Paul's great statement about Providence in the book of Romans: "We know that in everything God works for good with those who love him, who are called according to his purpose" (Rom. 8:28).

Long before Paul biblical writers took this point of view. Look at one of the poetic passages in Psalms:

> He who dwells in the shelter of the Most High,
> who abides in the shadow of the Almighty,
> will say to the Lord, "My refuge and my fortress;
> my God, in whom I trust."—Ps. 91:1-2

Christ brings us the same reassurance of God's care when he reminds us, "even the hairs of your head are all numbered." God watches even the sparrows—and men are of more value than birds. Therefore the thing to do is trust in God and have no more fears for safety (Luke 12:4-7).

What About Predestination?

"I'd like to look to God for strength and help," a blue-eyed blonde just beginning college remarked after church one day. "But with me there's no stopping point. If I look to God at all, I find myself forced to think of 'predestination.' That makes God a dictator and me nothing."

A hard view, indeed. But what did this girl mean by "predestination"? Most people associate the word with John Calvin, the sixteenth-century Reformer who inspired the Presbyterians. Too many of us think of Calvin as a gimlet-eyed, old Puritan who had ice water for blood. And we think of predestination—God's advance control of our destinies—as a cold denial of freedom.

Actually, John Calvin was a very warm theologian and he meant something comforting by predestination. "The will of God is the supreme and primary cause of all things," says Calvin. By this he means not to take away our freedom but to remind us that we may have rest and assurance only when we freely trust God and follow him.

"We shall never feel persuaded as we ought," says Calvin, "that our salvation flows from the free mercy of God as its fountain, until we are made acquainted with his eternal election." The thought that God has chosen us as his people should "deliver us from fear."

In fact, Calvin's interest in "predestination" and John Wesley's later interest in "assurance" aren't as far apart as some scholars have thought. Each man aimed to tell his people of God's care over them (Calvin perhaps in more passionate terms than Wesley), and each aimed to tell his people of their duty to respond to God's love through their own decisions and acts (Wesley perhaps using more passionate terms than Calvin).

48

Persistent Questions About Providence

But persistent questions still remain. Granted, evil is real. Granted further, it always represents, in some manner, God's work. Now: Does our trust of God mean we will surely be rid of the evil? Or does it mean we will have strength to endure the suffering?

The best answer is that it probably means both, to some degree.

One thing faith never guarantees us: that we will have to do *no* suffering. All of us have to suffer some of the time, and some people seem to suffer just about all the time.

Some people, it might be added, suffer unnecessarily. They do it either to test their faith needlessly, or because they simply aren't using their heads.

Faith tells us we can hope for the end of whatever evils plague us. Not now, perhaps. To take the example of the boll weevils again, there is no telling how many farmers went under financially before the shift from one crop to many crops was accomplished. These farmers suffered while the changes were taking place, and when the evil of the one-crop system had been lessened, it was too late to do some of them any good.

So our hope must never be tied too directly to the *here and now*. Still, we can hope confidently, knowing that God's way is going to win out in the end, and *perhaps* right now for others if not for us.

Faith also tells us we can try to avoid suffering up to a point. At the same time (as Bishop Aulén reminds us) "the prayer of faith for God's protection is not a prayer to

49

be delivered from suffering and grief, but a prayer that God will preserve us in *all* danger and harm, and above all that God's dominion may be realized."

It helps to remember Jesus' own prayer when he was faced with the suffering that would cost him his life. No one goes out and invites death for no good reason. No one takes on suffering pointlessly. Jesus therefore prays: "My Father, if it be possible, let this cup pass from me." (Matt. 26:39.) It was not possible; as events turned out, Jesus was called on to make the supreme sacrifice on behalf of his fellow men. We know he looked ahead to this possibility, because in the same prayer he added: "Nevertheless, not as I will, but as thou wilt" (Matt. 26:39).

Christians should make this same prayer. When we can enter into its spirit, we will have understood God's *Providence*. We will have also understood what prayer means.

WHAT DO YOU THINK?

1. In the far West grasshopper swarms often attack farms, cleaning every blade of grass off the soil. Can we really say such misfortunes are the work of Providence?

2. Suppose a member of a snake-handling cult cited the following Bible verse to you: "They will pick up serpents, and if they drink any deadly thing, it will not hurt them" (Mark 16:18). How would you interpret the verse?

3. Must a believer in Providence say that God directs every single event in his life?

4. Most of us know the stirring story of Dunkirk from World War II, where thousands of English soldiers were evacuated from France and saved from the Germans in what seemed

to many a miracle. Try to think of this event from the point of view of the Germans and then comment on how it represented Providence.

5. Can you think of instances in your own life or your own community when greater trust in Providence would have been justified?

6. One critic of predestination has said it is valid for an individual in explaining his own relation to God but a very wicked doctrine when applied to human affairs in general. Why do you think he made this statement?

7. What is the difference, in your conception, between predestination and Providence? Can you accept the old distinction that the former deals with "salvation," the latter with our fortunes in this world?

PART II

SIN

IV

Is Sin Here to Stay?

OLIVER TWIST, HERO OF DICKENS' NOVEL OF THE SAME name, was seemingly born to suffer. Left at the door of an orphanage as a baby, little Oliver was regarded as an unnecessary mouth to feed. He was no more than a child when the orphanage director turned him over to a funeral home for apprenticeship as undertaker's assistant.

At the funeral home Oliver was falsely accused of stirring up trouble, and he ran away—only to fall into the hands of Fagin, a master pickpocket. Against his will Oliver was then made to assist Fagin and his gang in criminal acts. Once a good man rescued Oliver and took him home with him—but not for long. Soon Oliver went out alone on an errand, and one of Fagin's associates seized him. Back in Fagin's control, the boy was again forced to act as an accessory to criminals.

Oliver Twist was the victim of the worst kind of evil—moral evil. He suffered at the hands of *men* rather than at the hands of *nature*. In the past three chapters we have examined "natural evil," or human suffering that comes from nature. Now we turn to a far more disturbing kind: moral evil or *sin,* a kind of evil by which men inflict the deepest suffering of all on themselves and their fellows.

How to Manufacture Evil

Man-made products often turn out to be better than the natural article. Tires of synthetic rubber, for example, can be made to yield more service than tires of natural rubber. Japan's silkworm industry has been outdistanced by America's synthetic fiber industries, for man-made cloth is superior in many ways to silk made from the cocoons of caterpillars.

In the same way, man seems to be far more efficient at creating evil than nature is. The blast of a hydrogen bomb may contain less energy than the winds of a tropical hurricane. Yet the mere threat of hydrogen warfare has already generated more anxiety and despair than all the hurricanes of history put together.

Why are men so expert at the creation of evil? Oddly enough, it is because we are so intelligent and creative and industrious—and free.

This reasoning may sound fantastic. After all, everyone has heard the old argument that the main trouble with men is their "ignorance" or their "lack of education." Civilize people and educate them, you often hear it said, and men will cease to be cruel to each other; they will become so interested in progress and democracy that they will forget about wrongdoing.

It just doesn't work out that way. The most effective forms of evil are those perpetrated by the cleverest minds. The more educated men become, the more capable of creating havoc they become. The more science-minded and industrialized a nation becomes, the more capable it becomes of creating mass suffering.

Take the problem of alcohol. The alcoholic is strictly a modern development. Although primitive societies had intoxicants, they didn't have the spare time that we do, and so they didn't make a sport or hobby out of drinking. More important, they didn't live under the pressures that we do, and they didn't have the industrial know-how for distilling alcohol efficiently. They just didn't ever have enough alcohol at once to get very many people very drunk.

It is different nowadays. We are clever enough to produce alcohol faster and in larger quantity than nature can do through fermentation. And with our large purchasing power and great amounts of spare time, the temptations of this available alcohol are just too much for many people. Result: alcoholism, a first-class evil—the product of man's intelligence, creativity, industriousness, and freedom.

Or take the matter of war. We moderns like to kid ourselves. We like to think we are less warlike than primitive tribes. Yet the fact remains that warfare didn't become an efficient, wholesale method of killing off entire populations until the twentieth century. Our atom bombs did more damage in one minute during World War II than any ancient tribe of barbarians could do in a whole day of pillage and rapine.

It was modern man—Communists and the Nazis—who showed how to make effective war against the minds and spirits of masses. Propaganda, more powerful in a deep sense than the hydrogen bomb, is something men have got the knack of only within the last few years, relatively speaking.

What of the Future?

An optimistic church woman recently wrote to the editor of her daily newspaper:

"I predict that church attendance will continue to grow and that crime will decline, as a result of the religious training the younger generation is receiving now."

As good as religious training is in some churches, it is hard to believe that sin, and therefore crime, is going to disappear any time soon. If we may accept the biblical view, we can draw a ready conclusion right away: Sin is a hard reality. It shows no signs of going away, and never has. In fact, all the evidence seems to point in the opposite direction.

The smarter we get, apparently, the more able we become to make trouble. The better men get at inventing and producing, modern history suggests, the more powerful they become in putting through evil schemes. In short, it would seem, the more we progress, the more we are tempted to use our progress for mistreating each other.

W. J. Cash has described the economic recovery brought to North Carolina after the Civil War through the growth of cotton mills.

Here, obviously, was hope for the South. . . . The head of a family, collecting wages for a wife and half a dozen children, had more cash in his pocket at the end of a fortnight than he had commonly seen on the land in a year.

And yet, along with this "progress" came misery—child labor, long working hours, unhealthful working conditions.

At six, at seven, at eight years, by ten at the latest, the little boys and girls of the mill families went regularly to work. . . . Wages were bad; the hours which had to be worked for them were bitterly long. . . . Sixty-eight to seventy-two hours each week. . . . Men and women and children were cooped up for most of their waking lives in the gray light of glazed windows, and in rooms which were never effectively ventilated. . . . A dead-white skin, a sunken chest, and stooping shoulders were the earmarks of the breed.

Not that sin is something new, a product of the Industrial Age. Far from it. Men have always been expert creators of evil, more adept at the manufacture of suffering than nature ever was.

We might even think of man as being a part of nature, representing nature in a highly specialized way. Though he was created by God, he knows himself to be formed by God "of dust from the ground" (Gen. 2:7). If nature, though God's good creation, still contains the possibility of evil, then we have to say that human nature, God's highest creation, contains the possibility of the most expert evil of all.

You find it hard to "sell" this point of view nowadays, but the Scriptures insist on it passionately.

Jeremiah, a man of acute insight who lived in a troubled period of Israel's history, points out over and over how men stubbornly insist on creating evil for themselves. Sometimes, it seems to this anguished prophet, each new generation is worse than the last. "Your fathers have forsaken me, says the Lord," Jeremiah once snorted at his countrymen, "and . . . you have done worse than your fathers." (Jer. 16:11-12.) Other great prophets, especially Amos and Isaiah, make similar statements.

Jesus, too, tells us the same thing. His followers call him "Lord, Lord," but they will not do what he tells them (Luke 6:46). Men will always have the opportunity and temptation to sin (Luke 17:1). Each generation, confronted with the hard demands of its Lord, seems to deserve the name "faithless" (Mark 9:19).

For every evil men manage to conquer, seven more evils arise to tempt them, and he who is not strong enough to resist is worse off in the end than he was before (Luke 11:24-26). Progress and education and knowledge, then, *increase* instead of *reduce* our temptations. If we have conquered the "one" evil of being primitive, in its place we now face the "seven" evils of being civilized.

Just one other point and we can rest our case for the reality of sin. Because so many of the sins of our time are spectacular *group* affairs, we are tempted to discount personal responsibility. War, for example, seems something that "nations" enter into. Yet Jesus reminds us that sin is always a personal matter. It is invariably from within, "out of the heart of man." Everything from evil thoughts to mass

60

murder has its beginning in men's souls (Mark 7:21-23).

In past chapters we have been discussing natural evil as somehow the work of God. Can we extend this point, and hold also that *sin* is God's creation in us, too?

Here even the strongest upholders of God's might put in a word of warning. John Calvin, the father of modern "predestination" declares: "The will of God is the supreme and primary cause of all things, and God holds the devil and the godless subject to his will." But in the very next breath he adds: "Nevertheless God cannot be called the cause of sin, nor the author of [moral] evil, nor subject of any guilt." This is true even though the wicked deeds of men may "justly and rightly be used to a good end."

No man can use God's will as an excuse for his sin, for God directs no one to sin. We manufacture moral evil for ourselves, and the factory is located within our own hearts.

Original Sin

If God does not require men to sin, perhaps he creates them as born sinners. At least, that is the suspicion of some.

Here, too, the Bible's point of view sets us on the right track again. God created man for fellowship with him, and genuine fellowship can be had only when the two parties involved cleave to each other voluntarily. So God created man with freedom to choose good or evil.

Man, in his freedom, seems inevitably to forget what his freedom is for. Drunk with what John Wesley called the "pride of life," we conclude that our freedom is for getting rid of God rather than for finding our way to him. So practically from birth each of us finds himself led astray

61

by his interest in himself. Even a new-born baby, though he is not conscious of what he is doing, arranges his life to meet what can only be called his self-centered needs. By the time he is old enough to choose, he is caught deep in the tangles of serving himself.

Reflecting on this habit into which we all grow, it is easy to agree with Wesley that we are all "born in sin." God does not make us that way—but we fall into the habit.

This inheritance of thinking first of ourselves is what we can call "original sin." It is our well-nigh invariable habit of using our talents and freedom to serve ourselves.

It's Not Hopeless

Let us not despair, however. God sees us fall victim to ourselves, and he comes to the rescue. Not by working on us magically, but by offering us a new spirit, courage, and energy. He cleans off our mottled and corroded freedom, so to speak, and lets us use it again.

This act of rescue God has accomplished through Jesus Christ. If we turn to Christ, admitting we have served only ourselves in the past, we can become new men.

Indeed, God's new offer of freedom points the way to hope for our whole society, not just for us as individuals.

It may be true, as we have seen, that the more civilized people become, the more their ability to sin increases. In that sense, knowledge, education, and science are new frontiers of evil.

It is equally true, however, that man *can* use his knowledge and creativity and power for *good* rather than evil. The more powerful and clever a nation or man becomes, the better the opportunity for good.

Primitive men could only sit by helplessly when disease struck. At best, they could resort to magic, which helped cure only psychologically. Civilization, with all its dangers, has brought healing knowledge. Just a few years ago, pneumonia or influenza could be fatal to a majority of the people on whom it got a stranglehold. Now, thanks to the drugs and know-how of medical science, neither disease is often fatal. You could multiply the examples endlessly.

Knowledge and science have truly freed us of some of the worst dangers and fears that have traditionally faced men. It is much easier to use these powers for wrong than for right, however.

Again, we can turn to the writers of the Old and New Testaments for insight.

We have already referred to Jeremiah's conviction that men stubbornly create evil for themselves. Now let us go further and see if we can find out why, according to Jeremiah, they do so. Speaking of the Hebrews, Jeremiah declares: "They did not obey or incline their ear, but walked in their own counsels and the stubbornness of their evil hearts, and went backward and not forward" (Jer. 7:24). Every man among them "follows his stubborn evil will," refusing to listen to God (16:12). The Hebrews find themselves engaged in the manufacture of troubles because, as they say, "We will follow our own plans" (18:12). Jesus says many similar things.

The Risk of Manhood

Jeremiah was a good judge of human nature. What he says about the Hebrews applies equally to us. It is just as hard for us to follow God's plans as it was for the Hebrews. Perhaps, in a way, it is even harder for us to follow—because our great progress has loaded us up with so many "successful" plans of our own that we are tempted to ignore God's.

For example, we take great pride in our ability to wipe out slum areas and replace the tenements with attractive low-rent housing projects. One famous project of this kind in Brooklyn, N.Y. contains housing for 3,500 families. Truly, we say, this is magnificent progress! But is it? This very housing project has become new slums, a center of vicious gang activity.

"Nowhere this side of Moscow," writes Harrison Salisbury of the *New York Times,* "are you likely to find public housing so closely duplicating the squalor it was designed to supplant."

Our main mistake, if this example is any evidence, is to believe that human effort alone does away with sin. It is a foolish notion. Life will never be that simple. The temptation to create evil is always with us, and the more civilized we become, the more the temptations multiply.

We have already discovered, in the past pages, that the very risk of living subjects us all to the perils of physical evil. Now, we must go on to say that the risk of being men, and especially civilized men, subjects us to the perils of moral evil. God gives us our freedom. If this freedom means anything, we will always be at liberty to sin. That is just what happens when we put all our faith in ourselves and our man-made schemes. Freedom used this way is freedom used against ourselves.

Yet we have hope against sin and its temptations. This hope comes from having faith in God. Even a little faith is enough to enable us to reclaim our imagination and science and knowledge and industry—and use them for good. For a mustard seed's worth of faith enables one to do what seems a miracle (Luke 17:5-6).

WHAT DO YOU THINK?

1. Lynching has almost disappeared in America. Does this show that men are less sinful now than they were in 1890 when lynching was widespread?

2. How much truth is there to the biblical statement: "He who increases knowledge increases sorrow"? (Eccl. 1:18.)

3. List some of the ways in which a society of civilized, Christian people can unwittingly enmesh individuals in sinful situations (as Oliver Twist was enmeshed—see introduction to chapter).

4. In the fifth century an optimistic British monk, Pelagius, was credited with the view that sin is "that which can be let alone." More than a thousand years later, Goethe remarked that sin is "that which *cannot* be let alone." Which view is nearer the truth?

5. Is it more truthful to say that sinful man finds God, or that God finds man despite man's sinful attempt to hide from God? Or must we say both?

6. Why is moral evil worse than natural evil? Why is sin more difficult to control than physical catastrophe?

7. An ancient theory of human nature holds that men are born naturally good, even with a spark of divinity implanted in them. Why does the Christian faith have trouble accepting this viewpoint?

V

The Wages of Sin

DURING THE OFF-SEASON, A MAJOR LEAGUE BASEBALL PLAYER suffered a broken back in an automobile accident. He was crippled for life. Never again would he even throw a baseball, much less play on the diamond.

The same year another major league baseball player spent his vacation fishing and golfing. Before he returned to his team for spring practice, he signed a big contract that made him a certain millionaire, if he handled his income well. Besides, he continued to enjoy perfect health and could probably look forward to ten more years in the national spotlight as a successful big-league star.

How do we explain the contrasting fortunes of these two men? Why was one condemned to a life of suffering and the other handed a life of wealth, fame, and success?

According to a very popular but false theory, you could confidently predict: Player A is a sinner; his suffering is God's punishment for his sins. Player B is righteous; his success is God's reward (or down payment) for his goodness.

Nothing could be further from the real teachings of Christianity than this theory. It is entirely false, if we are to accept the New Testament (and a great deal of the Old Testament).

Yet nearly all of us now and then lapse into acceptance of this false theory of suffering, in one form or another. It is all too easy for the modern Christian to convince himself that suffering comes only as a result of sin—especially when he is judging others—and that happiness and success, on the other hand, are sure signs of a virtuous life—especially when he is judging himself. In this chapter our object is to seek the real connection, if any, between sin and suffering—between the evil that man creates for himself and the misery he seems condemned to endure.

For Job, Poor Advice

The story of Job, as it begins, has God and Satan talking about Job (chs. 1-2). God tells Satan what an upright man Job is. Satan, always the skeptic, scoffs at this. He tells God, in effect:

"Job behaves uprightly only because he has all the advantages. Let me work him over, and you'll see how blameless Job is. Take away his comforts, and he'll curse you to your face."

God gives Satan permission to do his worst on Job, ordering him only to stop short of taking Job's life.

So Satan gives Job the works. A messenger comes to inform Job that a raiding party has killed his servants and carried off his livestock. Before this servant can get through

67

his message, another rushes up to tell Job his sheep have been killed by lightning, and the servants tending them also. A third dashes in about that time with the information that the Chaldeans have raided Job's camels, stolen them all, and killed the servants tending them.

Worse news is yet to come. Job's sons and daughters die in a great storm which blows down the house in which they are dining. Finally Satan afflicts Job with sores "from the sole of his foot to the crown of his head" (Job 2:7).

At this point, Job's wife is ready to give up, and she urges Job to do so. "Curse God, and die," is her desperate cry to him (Job 2:9).

Most of the rest of this powerful book goes into a conversation between Job and three of his friends who call to console him—and give him advice. Among them, they manage to give Job some of the worst advice a man ever had.

One of them, Eliphaz, sets out to explain to Job why he is suffering. You may read his exact words in chapter four, but for the moment, let's translate them into everyday English:

"I hope you won't be offended," says Eliphaz, "if I offer one little bit of advice here. In fact, it is impossible to keep silent. Now, Job, you are known as a strong man, and you have often helped the weak to stand up. With this kind of background, your troubles ought not to be very puzzling to you."

During all this, Job sits and listens. Eliphaz goes on.

"Don't you know that an innocent, upright man doesn't get into this kind of trouble? Plow iniquity, and you reap suffering. Misbehave, and God in his anger will do away with you." (Job 4:1-11.)

To Hebrews, this was an old, familiar argument. Not only men, but whole nations were subject to God's angry retribution. Even a man's sons, according to some of the more extreme views, could expect to suffer for their father's sins. The very Ten Commandments, supreme law of the people of Israel, subscribe to this theory. Those who worship graven images, we are told, will be punished, and what is more, so will their children "to the third and the fourth generation" (Exod. 20:5).

Job, however, will have nothing to do with the idea of retribution. He has already declared his attitude of trust. God offers us his hand, but that offer does not exempt his sons from risk-taking. "Shall we receive good at the hand of God, and shall we not receive evil?" (Job 2:10.) Still, he cannot understand why he should suffer so *much*. It is exactly the same thing we cannot understand today, though few of us are called on to undergo anything like the misfortune that Job bore.

After many more words among the three—and some memorable words from God—Job expresses regret that he has ever questioned God. He concludes that he had never known either God or himself fully until his suffering came upon him:

> I had heard of thee by the hearing of the ear,
>   but now my eye sees thee;
> therefore I despise myself,
>   and repent in dust and ashes.   —Job 42:5-6

69

Job finds himself by finding new faith in God, whom he now knows to be no tyrant. For the first time Job realizes he is much better off to have trust in God than to be proud of his own righteousness.

Here are some of the conclusions that we can draw from the story of Job:

1. Suffering is not to be explained as God's wrath against us for sin.

2. It is not a good idea for us to be too proud of our own righteousness, for the man who banks on his own powers might find them weak indeed in a day of trouble.

3. It is much better to put our faith in God and accept suffering along with blessings.

4. In that case, suffering will always seem a mystery, at least in part, but that view is much better than accepting a false explanation of suffering as punishment for sin.

Suffering and Sin

It is wrong, then, to say that suffering can be traced directly to God's wrath for our sins.

But can we say, on the other hand, that sin causes *no* suffering? Evidently not. Take some particular sin—addiction to narcotics, for example. Clearly enough, the participant in "dope" reaps a harvest of sufferings, not only for himself, but for everyone around him. So does the alcoholic or the merely selfish person.

Every time we turn against God, we turn in effect against ourselves. We deliberately set out to make trouble for ourselves, and usually succeed. So we cannot say that there is *no* connection between sin and suffering.

70

We have to come to a conclusion somewhat as follows then:

1. Not all suffering is the result of sin. We may suffer as a direct result of the good we do, for example.

2. But all sin results in suffering of some kind—mental, if not physical—for sin is a deliberate turning away from what is best in our lives.

The plain fact of the matter is that no one is likely to avoid suffering. Not even a saint can hope to—the saint, in fact, is probably the one who will never *try* to avoid it, but each of us can have a lot to say about the *kind of suffering* we do and about the effect it will have on us.

Every sincere Christian expects to be called on to suffer in the sense that we should bear one another's burdens and put service to God before personal comfort or safety. As Jesus reminds us: "If any man would come after me, let him deny himself and take up his cross and follow me" (Matt. 16:24).

Anyone who takes this warning seriously knows he will, in some sense, even have to give up his life: "For whoever would save his life will lose it" (Matt. 16:25).

If we try to avoid this kind of suffering, we may create for ourselves an even worse kind of suffering. To turn away from God and our fellows is to turn toward the dark, selfish world that Jesus calls the very opposite of "life" (John 3:36). In this world men give up their lives, too, as we are all warned: "Unless you repent you will all likewise perish" (Luke 13:5). Giving our lives to darkness is to lose life and to cut it away from God. Giving up our lives for others, however, is to find life and to join it to God.

Perhaps this advice seems idealistic. But we should remember that "giving up" our lives can start with the small and the practical. Let others talk while you listen. Offer to dry the dishes or clip the hedge—if it isn't already your job. Skip the business of claiming credit for your virtues once in a while.

The parents of a girl born with a crippled foot were asked recently: "Why don't you have the child's foot straightened by surgery?"

To which the parents responded: "God sent us this affliction because he is angry. If we had the foot straightened he'd find some other way of punishing us."

Who can accept this hard God? Christians who have absorbed very much of God's message can hardly argue that suffering is the result of God's angry punishment of sinners. It is true that some suffering is sent us by God simply because we live in a world that forces risk and chance and danger and death on one and all. A great deal more suffering also comes to us as the direct result of the evil we create for ourselves. But (as we shall find in the next chapter) God loves us in spite of the fact that we are sinners. Far from driving us away by his wrath, he constantly does his best to offer us his fellowship.

The wages of sin *are* death, but each person is his own paymaster. If we would let him, God would meet the payroll with life, not death.

What About the Hereafter?

After questioning ministers and theologians, an Associated Press writer concluded that more and more American Christians believe there is "no real fire in hell." He predicted: "There won't be nearly as much talk as there used to be about scorching flames and brimstone."

Convinced that no intelligent Christian can believe literally in hell (or heaven, either), a brilliant German theologian, Rudolf Bultmann, has proposed that we do away with both concepts.

It is old-fashioned now, Bultmann suggests, to consider heaven as "the abode of God and of celestial beings—the angels." The same thing can be said of the notion of an underworld called hell, "the place of torment." When the gospel builds on such elements, Bultmann declares, then it becomes "incredible" to modern man.

"No one who is old enough to think for himself supposes that God lives in a local heaven," Bultmann declares. "The same applies to hell in the sense of a mythical underworld beneath our feet."

These foundations of the old religion have fallen victim to scientific progress, in Bultmann's opinion.

Without judging Bultmann's theology, we can say that the evidence tends to confirm him on one point: fewer and fewer people take the idea of hell seriously.

Are we free, however, to reject part of our faith simply because it is no longer popular?

At this point, we need to remind ourselves what we have discovered so far in this chapter. We have concluded that God gives life to those who turn to him in faith; we have also concluded that God does not, on earth, inflict suffering as punishment for sin (because sometimes the innocent suffer while the wicked prosper).

Now we may ask, what is the situation beyond this life?

A veil of mystery immediately drops over the details, but we can be sure of one thing. The new life, for those who follow Christ, does not have to wait until *physical* death comes—it begins *now* (John 3:36). And the wages of sin, too, begin to be paid *now* rather than hereafter, for the man who turns himself over to sin is a walking manufactory of evil for himself, and he feels it inside him even while he treads this present round of existence.

The Bible expects us to believe that life continues somehow beyond the grave. Those who turn to Christ are assured that God will award them new life in the hereafter as well as now. Those who create evil for themselves are served notice that sin kills for good (Luke 13:5). Perhaps it is just as well for the individual to be left to supply the details for himself.

Some years ago the poet John Crowe Ransom complained that the trouble with American Christianity was its attempt to take God's "thunder" away from him. He referred to the frequent effort among moderns to convert God into nothing more than a divine cheerleader, enthusiastic about everything men do. A God who "thunders" sees that we are judged and is also mighty enough to protect us from our fears. So long as we restore to God his thunder, we do not need to be overly concerned that the old concepts of heaven and hell are changing. The essential thing is that we see God in control and therefore able to give us life in exchange for our present lives, a gift we may have instead of eternal death, if we follow him.

WHAT DO YOU THINK?

1. Since Job was a "righteous" man, why should he have been in need of humbling?

2. During a recession, a large factory lays off one thousand of its five thousand workers. Who is to blame, if anyone, for the suffering this imposes on the families of the laid-off workers? How should the management go about deciding which workers to lay off?

3. How might ancient Hebrews have interpreted the defeat of Germany in World Wars I and II?

4. Decide on the relation between sin and suffering in each of the following cases: (a) A professed atheist drags his daughter forcibly out of a church service. Twenty-four hours later, he is struck by a meteor and killed. (b) A drunken motorist rams a telephone pole and is maimed. (c) A drunken motorist collides with another car and escapes uninjured, but all the occupants of the other car are seriously hurt. (d) In a gang fight on city streets, two members of the gang are badly cut up; a passer-by is slugged from behind and crippled for life.

5. Some theologians, from the third century's Origen to the twentieth century's Nels F. S. Ferré, have rejected the idea that God consigns sinners to an eternal hell as punishment. What is your own feeling about the fate of those who reject fellowship with God?

6. Many moderns are convinced we should do away with the notion of "sin," holding that guilt feelings have no proper place in civilized society. How do you react to this suggestion?

7. Can one hold an idea of "sin" without believing in God? Can one believe in God without believing in sin?

VI

God's Answer to Moral Evil

In 1607 A HUNDRED AND TWENTY SETTLERS FROM ENGLAND
landed on a small peninsula thirty miles inland from the
mouth of the Powhatan or James River. This tiny Virginia
colony was the first permanently established settlement in
the United States.

Few of us realize the sufferings which these settlers en-
dured. When Sir Thomas Gates arrived in 1610 with more
settlers, he found the ranks of the Jamestown colonists
thinned down to a handful. The few who met him on the
wharf were half-starved, and some were out of their minds.

If we analyze the woes of the colonists, we find three
causes.

First, there were the physical difficulties of a new land.
The colonists didn't know how to farm under the new conditions. They had chosen a low, marshy district for living
quarters; disease hit them and killed or crippled many.

Second, the colonists feared the Indians. All around

them in the forests and waters were game and fish, but the settlers dared not venture out to take advantage of these resources.

Third, both the leaders and owners of the colony were bad managers and greedy as well. They insisted that the colonists devote their energy to shipping lumber and other cargoes back to England. This took so much time there was little opportunity for sensible farming operations. Dazzled by stories of gold Spaniards had mined in America, the proprietors expected the Virginians to get busy with mining operations instead of setting out corn and other crops.

When the colonists did begin their farming, they took a step that was to have dire consequences, for in 1619 Jamestown became the first place in the original thirteen colonies to introduce Negro slaves. Over two hundred years later, America would finally decide, through a bloody civil war, that slavery could not be the means of operating an economy.

Jamestown was an ill-fated colony through all of its days. The unhealthy terrain continued to claim lives, and the population was continually dwindling. Disastrous fires destroyed many of the buildings in 1608 and 1698. When the seat of government was moved to Williamsburg in 1699, the village of Jamestown fell into decay.

Deadly Combination at Jamestown

These troubles, we can see, stemmed from a combination of what we have been calling "physical evil" and "moral evil." Virginia's first colonists starved not only because nature was unfriendly, but also because of the greed of the colony's owners in England, the mismanagement of the colony's leaders, and the anxieties of the colonists themselves.

Most of the evil which men face is like that. It is a combination of these two kinds, physical and moral. We undergo a certain amount of hardship and danger because the world is built that way. We always make it worse for ourselves by the evil we ourselves create.

In his first letter to Corinth Paul describes this combina-of evils in a few short words: "The sting of death is sin" (I Cor. 15:56). We could face the world and all its terrors gloriously if we did not insist on making things worse for ourselves by selfishness, short-sightedness, and fear.

If we could conquer these lapses of the spirit, not even death itself would throw us into despair. If we could only use our freedom to meet our problems with imagination and faith, we could indeed say that death has no sting.

Let us not be too critical, however, of the Virginia colonists, or of their leaders and proprietors. All men have always been easy prey for their own shortcomings. As far as we can tell, men will always, in all probability, make evil a far more complex and terrible problem than it "naturally" is.

Our real enemy is not the hurricane, the epidemic, the famine, the threat of death. We can face all these perils. We can overcome many of them. We can meet the insoluble ones, like death, with courage. Our real enemy, the force that keeps us from a victory, is our inability to handle *ourselves*.

In short, the problem of suffering is in large part the problem of human sinfulness. The Virginia colonists found their perils complicated by three varieties of sinfulness, as we have seen: greed (on the part of the proprietors), pride (on the part of bungling leaders who supposed themselves capable), and despair (on the part of the colonists themselves when they feared to face the Indians).

These are not the only kinds of sins, but they illustrate the point pretty well. The sins of this year may vary in detail from those of the colonists, but underneath, we all are pretty much like the men of 1610—or those of any other age. Universally, men add to their sufferings because they fall into the grip of their own sins.

Find the answer to human sinfulness, and you go a long way toward finding the answer to the problem of suffering.

What Is a Sinner?

What is a sinner like? Basically, from the Bible's point of view, a sinner is someone who has turned aside from God. He is a man who prefers to listen to something else or someone else than God. Usually, this someone else is himself. A sinner is someone who puts himself before God. He may do so in selfishness, or he may do so in overconfidence, falsely relying on himself to perform the impossible. Or he may do so in fear, refusing to seek the strength God offers men.

The author of Psalm 36 has captured the spirit of the sinner. First, according to this revealing poem, the wicked man reserves the place deepest in his heart for "transgression" rather than for "fear of God" (Ps. 36:1).

79

Next, the sinner is a man who "flatters himself in his own eyes." He deceives himself into thinking no one knows he has turned away to serve himself (Ps. 36:2). He also deceives others, for "the words of his mouth are mischief and deceit," and it is no wonder that he ceases to "act wisely and do good" (Ps. 36:3).

Such a person spends all his time at his sin. It has become the most important thing in his life. Even while he is supposed to be asleep, "he plots mischief." He has turned away from God, in short, to himself, and he becomes a full-time producer of man-made evil. This passage comes close to describing all of us.

At this point, we must make sure of one distinction.

Men are not sinners because of their troubles. Rather, they are sinners because of the false solutions they attempt to use in attacking their troubles.

We refuse God's offer of help and tackle our problems all by ourselves—and we fall victims to the sin of pride.

We pay no attention to our neighbor's troubles but seek only to extricate ourselves—and we fall victim to the sin of selfishness.

We give in to the troubles, let them dictate terms of surrender; or we give up without trying to solve our troubles at all—and we fall victim to the sin of despair.

One further distinction: neither are men sinners because of their anxieties. It is what they *do* with their anxieties that counts.

Actually, everyone has worries and fears. You can use them wrongly or rightly. You can build a stockade around your life and refuse to venture out as the first settlers at

Jamestown did. That is the same as letting anxieties throw you into the sin of despair. Or you can forge ahead to improve the situation, driven to it in a healthy way by your anxieties.

Most of the frontier people who crossed over into Kentucky and Ohio had great anxieties about the wilderness, about the fearsome job of clearing the forests to make farming land. Yet the majority were driven to victory by these very anxieties. Having faith, the settler burned up his energy in clearing the wilderness, not in fretting about the dangers of the task.

Always, on every hand, the dangers of our lives threaten us. They are no longer the dangers of a frontier, but they are no less dangers. We fear what others will think. We worry about our financial situation. We fret over our health. The problems of existence continually try to trip us, and we are never more than one step from stumbling into despair.

It is not too strong, then, to say that sin is always at hand. At every moment we are potential if not actual sinners. And at every moment we are tempted to adopt false solutions to life—pride, selfishness, despair.

How Do We Escape?

How do we get out of this prison? Not by looking to ourselves, certainly. To return to Psalm 36, we can say that our only hope is God's "steadfast love," his "faithfulness" toward men he knows to be sinful, his "righteousness," and his "judgments" (which may be hard, but which we have to accept if we are to be restored to God's fellowship) (Ps. 36:5-6) .

Because God's steadfast love comes to us when we least deserve it, all men can take refuge with him. Indeed, if they are to overcome themselves, they *must* do so,

> For with thee is the fountain of life;
> in thy light do we see light. —Ps. 36:9

Overcoming sin, that is, can never be a simple matter of deciding to cut out a few bad practices and begin a few good ones. It is rather a question of turning ourselves completely over to God, in prayer and thought as well as action.

When we really accept God, death loses its sting. To be sure, we will die someday, just the same. But death is no longer such a threat if we can overcome *selfish* reasons for living; or the *pride* of thinking we shouldn't have to die, or the *fear* of knowing we will surely die.

The same goes for suffering. The thoughtful Christian does not really hope to avoid troubles and pain. As a matter of fact, he knows that by taking up his cross he is actually inviting peril, but he does hope for the strength to face his evil days and actually to overcome at least some of them. For this hope and strength he offers, as Paul puts it, thanks to God, "who gives us the victory through our Lord Jesus Christ" (I Cor. 15:57) .

Flying Upside Down

All this is easier said than done, mainly because we are quite unwilling, as a rule, to see ourselves as sinners.

In his book about the development of commercial airlines, Byron Moore tells of a frightening episode that befell Tom Hill, a pilot, in the days before instrument flying had been perfected. Flying a mail plane one night from Chicago to Detroit, Hill ran into thick clouds. He could see neither the sky nor the ground.

Then he began losing altitude. He had to land somewhere in a hurry. Hoping to locate an open field, Hill threw a lighted flare out of the plane. To his utter amazement, however, the flare seemed to fall not down, toward the ground, but *up*.

In a split second Hill realized what had happened. His instruments had failed, and in the clouds he had gradually banked his plane into upside down flight without knowing it. To save his life he now had to go against his instincts and turn his ship into what seemed the opposite of right side up.

Moore reports that the pilot barely got his ship righted before he slammed violently into the ground. If Hill had heeded his own natural inclinations, he would have landed on his head and killed himself.

Most of us, in our everyday lives, are just as unaware of turning away from God as Tom Hill was of turning away from the ground. Part of our stance as sinners comes from the very fact that we simply cannot realize how upside-down our lives are most of the time. Just as the pilot had to make a resolute decision to act against what his instincts told him, overcoming sin means making a resolute decision against what "human nature" tells us.

The author of the Gospel of John suggests that the opposite of "sinner" is "believer in Christ" (John 16:9).

That might not be a bad way to think of the problem of sin. We will never overcome sin by our own righteousness. We will never overcome it by doing a few things or by not doing a few other things. God's answer to man-made evil is that we should turn ourselves over to Christ, the man who conquers evil. We can never eradicate the threat of sin as long as we are human beings, but we can fight a winning battle with Christ's help.

So far we have established that men know and undergo two kinds of evil, both of which cause suffering: physical evil and moral evil. We have learned that the Christian expects to face both kinds of evil, but that men can hope to lessen the moral evils they create for themselves. From here we will go on to consider the reality of suffering, the value of suffering, and, in conclusion, a Christian point of view toward the whole question.

WHAT DO YOU THINK?

1. Analyze the elements of (*a*) physical evil, (*b*) moral evil of various kinds in the following causes of suffering: the Korean War, the six-hundred-odd deaths on the highway that may attend the Christmas holiday period, perennial famines in India.

2. Some modern-day theologians, such as Reinhold Niebuhr, have suggested that all sinfulness can be reduced to one basic sin: pride. Do you think so? If not, what would you substitute for pride as the leading sin?

3. Can sin be eradicated? Does anyone ever sin without knowing it? Is it sinful to have anxiety?

4. Unlike the Jamestown colonists the Quakers who settled

Pennsylvania underwent no period of near starvation. Does their better fortune represent any higher evaluation placed on them by God?

5. How would you interpret the following statement of Paul's? "For I do not do the good I want, but the evil I do not want is what I do" (Rom. 7:19). Does this describe everyone? Yourself? Your minister?

6. Is sin a state or a series of acts? Why? What is the Bible's definition of sin?

7. Do you believe in capital punishment?

PART III

SUFFERING

VII

The Cup of Sorrow

WHEN AN ATOM BOMB FELL ON HIROSHIMA IN 1946, NEARLY 100,000 Japanese died. In addition, untold thousands found themselves condemned to living death. These were the wounded—victims of radiation, concussion, heat, and fire.

In many ways the worst sufferers of all were young girls not injured enough to die, but horribly disfigured. As they grew into young women old enough to marry, the depth of their tragedy became more apparent.

One eight-year-old girl, for example, was trapped in a burning schoolroom on the day the bomb fell. Ten years later her burns had healed, but they left her face a mass of dark, lumpy scars. At eighteen what hope did she have of marriage?

Another girl suffered burns on her arms, which became so disfigured from scar tissue that she always wore long gloves. Others entered adolescence with stiffened legs, crippled fingers, shrunken skin, and discolored flesh. The skin around one girl's forehead contracted so much in healing that she couldn't close her eye, and for ten years she slept by placing a black cloth over it at night.

Fortunately for some of these girls the story does not end here. Editor Norman Cousins of *The Saturday Review* led a movement to bring twenty-five of the disfigured to the United States for plastic surgery. American surgeons were glad to donate their professional services gratis. Many other citizens helped by giving money or by taking in the girls to live with them while they underwent the long process of painful operations needed to restore their looks.

The "Hiroshima Maidens," as these girls are universally known now, returned to Japan with better hopes. Not all their scars were gone—some of the twisted flesh could not be repaired by the best surgeons in the world. But all the girls looked better, and some went home as good as new.

These maidens live as compelling examples of the fact that suffering is horribly *real*. Whenever we are tempted to approach the subject of suffering as an intellectual matter, or as a topic for speculation only, we will do well to think of these scarred, disfigured girls. Their suffering was anything but imaginary.

Thinking of such victims, the Christian knows he cannot shun the burden of suffering. Even if he is fortunate personally and gets off easy, he still cannot escape: For other men's woes are his own, just as the tragedy of the Japanese bomb victims became a personal responsibility of the courageous editor of *The Saturday Review*. Indeed, the Christian's only hope of overcoming evil rests squarely upon his acceptance of evil's reality.

Two Kinds of Suffering

Our discussion of evil in the past six chapters gives us a lead and suggests the conclusion we may now reach about suffering.

We began by considering the matter of *physical* evil. We decided that creation would be incomplete without floods, storms, epidemics, and other challenges hurled by nature to men. The very basis of progress, we discovered, lies in man's courageous fight against the hard realities of nature.

Then we moved on to consider the reality of *moral* evil or sin. From the day men first drew breath, we found, they have tended to turn against the God who gave them breath. The result was, is, and seemingly ever shall be the production of man-made evil. By their refusal to heed God's word, human beings have always complicated their problems by their own selfishness, pride, and fear.

Now we can make a very similar statement about suffering. For, after all, suffering is the direct result of the two kinds of evil we discussed in earlier chapters. Some of it is caused by physical evil and some by sin. *Brave and thoughtful men know they will always face suffering*—a certain amount of it seems to be a "natural" part of their world, and even more of it seems to be brought on themselves by their own capacity to go astray.

Of these two kinds of suffering the more tragic clearly is the kind we create for ourselves. Take the Hiroshima maidens once more. Japanese anxieties and selfishness helped bring on World War II. American retaliation, empowered by brilliant achievements in the field of atomic

91

research, was perhaps brutal beyond the requirements of the situation. Result: a hundred thousand deaths in a single bomb blast and lifelong disfigurement for the maidens—who as mere children were about as innocent as any war victims you could name. For this evil we all share the guilt—Japanese, German, Briton, and American alike.

Another tragic consequence of the Hiroshima bombing was the arrest in 1959 of Major Claude Eatherly, forty, on charges of robbing a drive-in grocery in Dallas, Texas. Eatherly was the World War II pilot who scouted Japan in a B-29, found clear weather over Hiroshima, and returned to lead in another B-29, this one carrying the atomic bomb.

Blaming himself in later years for the deaths of the Japanese in the blast, Eatherly suffered mental and emotional stress, turned to crime. In 1956 he was accused of helping burglarize two government post offices in Texas and was acquitted on grounds of insanity.

Three years later, following his latest arrest, Eatherly was committed to a government hospital for treatment. Like the Hiroshima maidens he was the victim of man-made evil, but his suffering was possibly even more profound than that of the maidens, for the Hiroshima bomb shattered Claude Eatherly's spirit rather than his body.

Why Harp on It?

The thoughtful reader may ask, however: Why make so much of the reality of evil, sin, and suffering? Why not look for the better side of things?

That is a reasonable demand. Christianity is not a long-faced, mournful religion. Instead it is good news of God's interest in man. And the Christian, when he thinks of the meaning of his faith, can only be optimistic about the outcome.

However, it is a trait of human nature that we are rarely interested even in good news unless we have some way of seeing what it means, of understanding what it is intended to do. If Christian faith is in some way an answer to the problem of suffering, then we must first of all clearly see how suffering involves us all.

Accordingly, Scripture goes to great length to point out to us the hard facts. It aims, on almost every page, to force men to realize the desperate situation they are in. The Bible insists that we recognize the problem we face as the first step toward overcoming it. Only when we are well acquainted with the sober reality—that we human beings create evil and suffering for ourselves—can we take the big step toward freedom, the step of turning to God.

Suffering is real and always to some degree self-created. That is one of the messages of the Christian Scriptures.

Why should it be necessary for the Scripture to point this out? After all, pain is a physical fact. Medical men have even made some progress in measuring it. Any encyclopedia outlines the manner in which nerve endings protect the body by reporting with pain whenever our tissues or organs are endangered.

But the Bible means to convey far more than the physical reality of pain. Suffering, especially the self-created kind, is always inward more than external, spiritual more than physical, a sensation of the heart rather than of the nerve endings.

You get no further than the third chapter of Genesis before you come across a powerful reminder of the inner, self-created character of suffering. The story of Adam is the story of what goes on inside every man—in fact, the Hebrew word "Adam" actually means "everyman." God created man and offered him fellowship, but man, in his freedom, turned away from God and toward the dust of which he was created.

Adam, the first man—who really is best thought of as *every* man—created a world of pain and suffering for himself by his stubborn insistence on managing his own righteousness. Though this realm includes physical pain and outward suffering, it is primarily a world of stricken spirit, where suffering is most real at the core of the personality.

Because Adam has chosen it, he reaps evil and unnecessary suffering. God tells Eve, the woman, of the pain she shall ever endure in giving birth to more men. God tells Adam, the man, how he shall ever find the earth "cursed" because of his rebellious spirit. What he wins from the earth will come at the price of blood, sweat, and tears:

> In the sweat of your face
>   you shall eat bread
> till you return to the ground,
>   for out of it you were taken;
> you are dust,
> and to dust you shall return.
>   —Gen. 3:19

Remember, when the authors of Genesis speak of "Adam" they mean *you* and every man. When they speak of "Eve," they mean *life* ("Eve" is Hebrew for "life") and

THE CUP OF SORROW

every one who draws breath or passes life on to children. Every one of us, the author of Genesis seems to be saying, can expect to suffer as a result of a basic stubbornness— for every one of us seemingly tries to "go it alone," sooner or later, refusing the help God offers.

The suffering promised here by God is *not* punishment for sin—at least it is not God's punishment. The whole point of the Genesis story is to make it clear God wants man in fellowship with him, and that separation from God and the resulting evil is man's freely chosen preference.

The New Testament, too, goes to great length to point out that men must suffer. Even Jesus, because he is willing to share with men their human nature, found blood, sweat, and tears waiting for him. The night he was betrayed by Judas and arrested by the Jews, he retired to Gethsemane, where "he began to be sorrowful and troubled" (Matt. 26:37) . The sinless man who came to take away the world's sins chose to suffer as a man, like all men.

New Meaning for Pain

And yet, with the coming of Jesus Christ upon the scene, suffering takes on a new meaning.

First of all, we find in Christ a promise of help against *unnecessary* suffering. If with Adam all men turned away from God, then with Christ all are invited to turn back to him. As Adams all, we men create evil by our own selfishness, pride, and fear, but as followers of Christ we receive the hope of putting away these evils and inflicting them on ourselves no more. On our own we are certain to reject

God's fellowship; through Christ we find the door open once again.

Second, we find in Christ a promise of help against *necessary* suffering. Not that the follower of Christ can expect to be let off the hook. Those who follow him, as Jesus told the disciples, must be "able to drink the cup that I am to drink" (Matt. 20:22). This is not a cup of ambrosia; it is a cup of bitters.

Christ's followers must be, like him, willing slaves of humanity, bearers of the burdens of men, "even as the Son of man came not to be served but to serve, and to give his life as a ransom for many" (Matt. 20:28).

Even the necessary kind of suffering will pass, we believe. The Christian's exodus from self-interest leads through the wilderness of service to a promised fellowship with God. As Jesus told the doubtful Peter: "And every one who has left houses or brothers or sisters or father or mother or children or lands, for my name's sake, will receive a hundredfold, and inherit eternal life" (Matt. 19:29).

We need not sell this promised "eternal life" short, however, by thinking of it only as "pie in the sky." Eternal life, if it means anything at all, means something *right now*. Even while the Christian faces the problems of this world, he can begin to have his sample of eternity. The people who labored to see something done for the Hiroshima maidens must have seen partly through right then to eternity. By bearing their share of the guilt for hurting and the responsibility for helping the girls, these people must have already begun to receive their reward.

Certainly the girls themselves were able to grasp this

mystery, to see how God offers his fellowship in the midst of troubles. Gloria and Peter Kalischer, author of a magazine article about the maidens, reported the reaction of one of the girls:

"Why did former enemies treat us like daughters? When I wanted to ask this question I couldn't speak enough English, and later when I could, it didn't seem to matter any more."

WHAT DO YOU THINK?

1. Does a person, by attempting to heed God's word in his life, reduce his suffering—or does he increase it?

2. If Jesus was sinless, why should he have suffered? Was it distasteful to him to think of giving up his life? (See Mark 14:32-42.)

3. Is the deliberate seeking of pain a truly Christian motivation? Why or why not?

4. Why is inward suffering often more shattering to the personality than physical suffering?

5. Why must the Christian faith, basically a joyful religion, make so much of suffering?

6. Augustine argued that all men are sinners because Adam's sin was passed on through the procreation of children. Modern theologians are much more likely to argue that "Adam" means each of us rather than some remote ancestor. Which theory is the sounder? What are the strong and weak points of each theory? Is there a better explanation than either of these? Must we talk about "original sin," anyway?

7. How would you describe the difference between "necessary" and "unnecessary" suffering?

VIII

Why Suffer?

FOR STEALING A LOAF OF BREAD, JEAN VALJEAN WAS sentenced by a French court of law to prison and hard labor. He spent nineteen years in chains, pulling the oar of a galley.

After he had worked out his sentence, Valjean was cut away from his chains by the authorities and sent back into the world of free men. But still, he was not a free man. From then on, he would be a marked man, living under the harsh eye of the authorities and the suspicions of society. If he ever made a single slip in his conduct, he would go back to the galleys.

Rather than face this lifetime marked as an ex-prisoner, Jean Valjean changed his identity. Good fortune was with him, and within five years he had successfully built a new life as "Monsieur Madeleine." He became a prosperous manufacturer and was even chosen by the citizens of his community as mayor.

Now, he told himself, he would suffer no more. Neither the threat of physical servitude as galley slave nor the prospect of living as an outcast faced him any longer. He was a free man once more.

Then, something happened to make Valjean voluntarily let himself in for all these old sufferings once more. A demented old man who resembled Valjean was arrested by the French authorities; they had mistaken him for Valjean. The old man was brought to trial as a parole breaker. He was certain to be shipped to the galleys.

The real Valjean—Monsieur Madeleine to the world, now—could not allow this to happen. Madeleine appeared in court and revealed himself as the convict who had broken parole.

Why do men like Jean Valjean—the hero of Hugo's nineteenth-century novel, *Les Miserables*—seem to court hardship and suffering?

In Valjean's case he could have gotten away with his change of identity. The old man mistaken for him was not sane enough to convince the authorities of their tragic mistake. Most men in Valjean's place might have allowed the old man to go to the galleys. Indeed, that would have assured the real Valjean of permanent security, for the case of Jean Valjean, wanted criminal, would have been closed for good.

Instead of safety Valjean chose risk. Instead of happiness and wealth he deliberately chose danger. Valjean believed that a life of getting and taking was worthless; life could be of value only if it consisted of giving. When he found himself about to take away the freedom of an old man—even a worthless old man who didn't have good sense—Valjean answered by giving up his own success.

"Boundary Situations"

Valjean's life shows us how false it is to think of happiness and suffering as opposites. Life takes its meaning, in fact, from its crises or difficult moments. Karl Jaspers, a contemporary German philosopher, believes that there are several kinds of these crises in everyone's life, and that the man who is not ready to accept them is missing the deepest elements of living.

These crises Jaspers describes as "boundary situations." In each of them a man feels himself at the *limit* or *boundary* of his powers. Not until he reaches them does he know his own depths. And, a Christian might add, not until he reaches them does he fully realize his need for God's help.

What are the main "boundary situations" which reveal to a man the real significance of his life?

1. *Death:* One of these boundaries—the most obvious one to any of us—is *death*. Each of us must die. When we admit that we all face this limit, we take life more seriously. On the other hand, when we try to pretend there is no such thing as death, we cheapen life, rob it of its importance.

Many newspaper reporters do their best work when they face a *deadline*. They pursue facts more vigorously. They waste less time getting their stories written. They take themselves and their jobs more seriously.

The threat of death has something of this effect on all men. We know we work under a deadline. Therefore we pursue life more vigorously. We spend more time doing

100

what is really important. We take ourselves and our duties to others more seriously.

Jean Valjean must have strongly felt the boundary of death when he heard of the old man's trial. He could not allow the success of his own life to hasten another's death, nor could he overlook the impending threat of his own death. He would not cheapen the time he had left by buying happiness at such a price.

2. *Chance:* Another of the chief "boundary situations" is *chance.* Every one of us is subject day and night to the laws of chance. When we admit that the future is uncertain, we take the present more seriously. On the other hand, when we try to build a wall of security around our lives, we discount opportunities to live with courage and bravery.

A professional tightrope walker once missed his step and plunged thirty feet. He was not seriously injured, but from that day on he did not dare attempt his specialty again. For years he wandered from town to town as a panhandler. Finally, he met a friend who had confidence in him. The friend talked him into taking the risk of walking the high wire again. The former professional shut his mind to the danger and succeeded. Because he was willing to take a chance, he found himself again.

"Life cannot be played without stakes," says Gabriel Marcel, a French philosopher; "life is inseparable from some form of risk."

Jean Valjean was willing to take risks. He threw over his career as manufacturer and his post as mayor. He deliberately put himself outside the law, all because his personal creed of *giving* required it.

3. *Conflict:* A third "boundary situation" is *conflict.* The person who *believes* in something is certain to run into opposition, to encounter conflict. It may not always be in the form of *physical* conflict, but on the other hand, it is the conflicts of ideas or beliefs that put us to the strongest test. A great many Christians have found it necessary to engage in both physical and intellectual conflict in order to uphold their beliefs.

In 1517 Martin Luther was a young and promising Catholic priest in Germany. By "being a good fellow," keeping his mouth shut, and not rocking the boat, he could have become an important figure in the established Church of his day. Yet he believed that ordinary men were being deprived by this church of their right to worship Christ in freedom; his belief was so strong he felt he had to enter into conflict with nearly the entire Church. The result of his struggle with the Catholic hierarchy was the emergence of Protestant faith as we know it.

Jean Valjean threw off his role as Monsieur Madeleine and came in conflict with French authority for the rest of his life. Yet he had to—he could do no other. His belief in *giving* was far more important to his life than his love of peaceful existence.

4. *Pain:* A fourth "boundary situation" is the undergoing of *pain.* No one can escape it. Everyone faces physical, mental, or emotional pain, or perhaps all three. The person who avoids pain at any price is really avoiding life itself. Not that we should *seek* pain—Jesus certainly did

not do so, having asked God just before his crucifixion: "My Father, if it be possible, let this cup pass from me" (Matt. 26:39). Nevertheless, he went on, "not as I will, but as thou wilt" (Matt. 26:39). Men do not know themselves as followers of Christ, or even as men, until they take something of the same attitude.

Jean Valjean was not especially anxious to give up his life as Monsieur Madeleine. He would not have thrown over his princely manufacturer's income or his favored status as mayor unless there had been a compelling reason. We see a measure of his largeness as a man in his decision. What he stood for was more important than these two painkillers, wealth and social standing.

5. *Guilt:* The fifth of the "boundary situations" which Jaspers outlines is *guilt.* Here, too, we must include everyone. As long as men are men and not gods, they will be less than perfect. They will rebel against the God who gave them life and mistreat their brothers with whom they share life. Men do not know themselves as men, Jaspers hints, until they accept personally their share of the guilt for these shortcomings.

Indeed, it is in conceding guilt that men find their way out of guilt. The man who is sure he is a saint is surely not a saint. The real saint is the man who admits his selfishness, pride, and fear—and turns to God for help. Read the lives of some of the men Christianity has acclaimed as saints, and you will see how each of them has passed through this boundary situation. Augustine, for example, committed wilder sins than many a barbarian, but he found a way through them by his willingness to say before God how unsaintly he really was.

Jean Valjean found himself crushed under the guilt of causing another man's condemnation. At first, being merely human, Valjean tried to pass off the guilt and tell himself he would not intervene in the crazy old man's trial. He could not ignore the old man's situation, however, or his own responsibility for it. In the end, he stepped boldly into the courtroom and announced: "He is not the man whom you seek; it is I. I am Jean Valjean!" Could you have done so?

The New Testament's Version

In a famous sermon preached for his disciples and other listeners, Jesus tells us of these same "boundary situations," or difficulties which make or break a man's life.

Poverty is one of these situations, according to Jesus. If you can accept it, it is a blessing. The man who is willing to do without has found "the kingdom of God" (Luke 6:20).

In the same way hunger is a boundary situation. Not just physical hunger, but the hunger for all kinds of security can prove a false stimulus. Satisfy these false hungers, and you still have not satisfied life's deepest hunger. Master these false hungers, and "you shall be satisfied" (Luke 6:21).

So it is for those who weep—in the end they shall laugh (Luke 6:21). Those who give up a good name, if they have to, for their beliefs, will finally rejoice (Luke 6: 22-23).

Those who fill themselves, gloat on their success, seek to avoid pain, and prize popularity, all without a twinge of conscience—these will not truly find life. All that is waiting for them is "woe" (Luke 6:4-26).

The man who finds life must expect to love his enemies, do good, and lend, "expecting nothing in return." That man's reward, realized in his own life, "will be great" (Luke 6:35). Jean Valjean discovered this truth and willingly faced the "boundary situations" of his life. So must we if we are to capture anything lasting.

"I'm out of luck, I guess," a college student sighed after seeking employment for the summer. "I tried a half dozen places, and they all said they were looking for experienced help. The only thing I'm experienced in is borrowing money from my father."

Few words in the English vocabulary have departed further from their original meaning than "experience." Today we take experience to be the accumulation of skill or know-how, or the piling up of many years of service in a given type of work. But "experience" is based on the Latin "periculum"—peril or danger. To have *experience* in the literal sense of the word is to take life intensely with all its risks and dangers.

It's not going too far, then, to say that God wants *experienced* followers. That is, he wants us to meet life rather than shy away from it—to accept head on the *periculum* or peril of courageous living.

WHAT DO YOU THINK?

1. Under what conditions can poverty be a blessing? When is it a curse?

2. In a time when few Americans face actual starvation, what relevance has Jesus' declaration: "Blessed are you that hunger now, for you shall be satisfied"? (Luke 6:21).

3. Of the five "boundary situations"—death, chance, pain, guilt, and conflict—which do you think is the most terrifying? Which is the commonest? Which is avoided most? Are there other boundary situations? Name some.

4. List several modern "Jean Valjeans," men who have willingly faced the "boundary situations" in order to give to others and to make their own lives more acceptable to themselves. Review your own past experience with each of the five boundary situations.

5. What are the most flagrant instances of correctable suffering in your community today?

6. A frequent goal of modern religious education has been to provide children with plenty of "ideal experiences," showing how life can avoid excessive conflict. What criticism can you make of this attempt? What good do you see in it?

7. Why is the real saint likely to be a person who considers himself a sinner?

IX

The Moment of Victory

IN SPITE OF THE LEGEND THAT "AMERICA HAS NEVER LOST A war," few historians would claim now that the United States really won the War of 1812. Rather, this conflict ended as a draw.

True enough we did win some battles. In the most spectacular of these Andrew Jackson soundly defeated the British invasion force that had been sent to capture New Orleans. General William Henry Harrison repulsed the British and Indians in the Northwest, and American sea forces inflicted humiliating defeats on the proud British navy.

On the other hand, the British did us about as much damage as we did them. American invasions of Canada, plotted as a major U.S. strategy of the war, were failures. Three American armies tried it. Though one did briefly capture and burn the capital of Canada, all fell back well within American territory before the war was over.

The British, during this war, succeeded in the boldest invasion of American territory every attempted by a foreign power, for a British army sailed right up to our middle Atlantic coast, landed, routed a larger American force, then captured and burned Washington.

In the peace treaty worked out by British and American commissioners at Ghent in 1814 not a foot of land changed hands. Neither side was able to exact any drastic concessions from the other. At the end of the war each nation was just about where it stood before the war started.

"Invisible" Victory

Yet, even without a military victory, America soon discovered that she had won in another way.

One of the main issues over which America went to war was the highhanded attitude of the British Navy. English ships made a practice of halting and searching American ships. Whenever the English found a former British citizen on one of these ships, they were likely to make him a prisoner and force him to become a sailor in the British Navy.

It was this audacious policy of impressment that tipped the scales toward war. The United States had set out to force England to discontinue this search and seizure policy which cost many an American citizen, formerly British, his newly won liberty.

The Treaty of Ghent makes no mention of impressment. Seemingly, the war was useless, for America evidently failed to bring the objectionable British practice to a halt.

Yet, within relatively few years after the War of 1812 the British Navy changed its policies greatly. Thanks to American courage in taking on a superior naval power, this unfair practice soon disappeared from the high seas. Eventually all American citizens, including those of British birth, were safe from impressment.

To put it another way, America won a delayed victory in the War of 1812. This victory was invisible at the time of the peace treaty. In fact, considering that we failed to get the British to agree to cease impressment, it seemed at first that the war was a failure.

The point is important because it illustrates a central truth of the Christian attack on evil. In past pages we have seen how evil, sin, and suffering are hard realities. Because men are men, we seem to be fighting a losing battle against ourselves and the powerful evil forces men create and unleash on each other.

However, in the same way that America won an eventual victory in the War of 1812, the Christian knows that his faith has won ultimate victory over the forces he fights. We can even date the moment the battle was won.

Evil's Downfall

That moment of victory was Christ's death on the cross. At that point evil was defeated for all time. To be sure, it was an "invisible" victory at the time. To the bystanders who watched on that day, all seemed to be lost. Jesus of Nazareth, who had come to tell men of a new way to God, was put to death as a criminal. His followers were thrown into shock and despair.

Within three days, however, these same followers knew Christ had triumphed, not only over the Jewish religious leaders and the Roman civil officials, but over death itself.

109

We have a record of the faith of these followers in the four Gospels of the New Testament.

These followers soon testified, to themselves and to others: "The Lord has risen indeed" (Luke 24:34). What had first seemed a defeat now seemed a victory. God was mighty enough to bring the dead to life. As he had raised Christ, so he would raise those who followed Christ.

Not that Christ's rising would put an end to all evil, sin, and suffering on the spot, then and there in the year A.D. 33. We know nothing of the sort happened; today, we face evil just as men did before Christ went to the cross.

In other words, the war is still going on. It is not ended even yet, but the *victory* has been won. God promises life to those who follow Christ. Those who follow him have to follow him through the fight against evil, and that is why we are not surprised to find suffering still very much with us.

Yet we know now, thanks to Christ's victory over death, that victory awaits us, too.

The Christian's war against the evil in himself and in the world is not like a military war. The Christian can take comfort in the fact that the peace treaty has been worked out and signed *before* the war is over. That is what makes the Christian's war so different. We still have the battles to fight, but the outcome is assured. Satan has already signed an unconditional surrender. Still, every man must work his way through the perils of life in order to realize this victory.

How Does Christ Help Us?

Just what does Christ's victory amount to, though? How does it come to the individual?

"What you Christians seem to be driving at," a skeptical physics professor once argued, "is this: by his bravery and obedience Jesus set you a good example. But if that is the case, you make far too much of Jesus. I can name dozens of brave, humble men in history: Socrates, Buddha, and Mahatma Gandhi, to mention three. Why don't you worship them, also?"

Is that all Christians see in Christ? Was he merely a living model of proper conduct? If so, then he deserves not worship, but only admiration.

At the other extreme many of Christ's followers have wanted to make him into a heavenly magician. Christ frees us of our sins, we hear from this camp of believers, by a sort of hocus-pocus. Just as he turned water into wine, he turns men into saints. Some spokesmen for this point of view even go so far as to suggest that belief in Christ will correct physical defects in our bodies.

Beyond doubt, there is truth in both of these views. On the one hand, Christ *does* come to us as an example. If we worship God in the same way Jesus did, we may be sure, we will be closer to God. On the other hand, we can also believe that Christ does things for us that we could never do for ourselves, even on the strength of a good example. We should resist the theory that Christ is a magician, healing us while we sit still, but we must insist that he heals us in some way with our active cooperation.

Put in the simplest terms, Christ's help comes to us in this way:

First, he helps us as a man, as a brother. His personality shows us what life is like, lived under God's care. He *is*

111

our example, the example of genuine manhood which has come up to what it really can be.

Second, he helps us as more than a man, as God's son. Because God lived in Christ our brother, we can honestly say that God has come to live with us. Here Christ becomes far more than an example; he becomes the member of the family who introduces a *new kind of life.*

This new life sets us free from all the things which keep us from being men. It makes us, finally, into new men, real men, men of the same kind Christ is. This new life helps us actually to become the kind of men which we see in the example of the man Jesus.

So faith in Jesus Christ does two things for us. First, it gives us an example—a picture of what real manhood is. Second, it gives us help so that we can *become* real men.

What are some of the signs of this new life? How does it differ from the old life?

In the first place, we are liberated from having to rely on ourselves. Our confidence focuses no longer on our own schemes and plots for success. It centers no longer in the world of new clothes, higher salaries, and ever larger barbecue pits for the back yard. The Christian can enjoy the things of his world without relying on them for his well-being.

Second, the new life in Christ releases us from the claims of the moment. We no longer have to have everything here and now. It lets us take it easy at the stop light instead of growling inwardly while we wait for the light to turn green.

Third, the new life turns our attention to others. Into

112

the vacuum created when we discount ourselves, God pours our neighbors and their problems. They become our responsibility, just as we have become Christ's.

Fourth, the new life makes us *use* our freedom and talents. God does not hand us his blessings on a silver platter. His help fades out and becomes invisible to the person who does not decide to do something with it.

Fifth, the new life shows us an open, unlimited future instead of a closed, death-filled one. The pain of life and the prospect of death stop us only if we love darkness; but he who puts his faith in Christ "comes to the light" (John 3:21). Everything becomes possible—not even the certainty of our own death can stand in the way, for we can see possibilities beyond death.

Christian faith will not make us into wizards, of course. We will not immediately realize all of these features in our lives. But in following Christ, we will realize some of them all the time and all of them at some time.

Was Jesus a "Success"?

Knowing all this changes the Christian's idea of what "success" means. We can say that "success" in the deepest sense may seem "defeat" *at the moment*. We can also say that "success" does not mean "absence of suffering." The greatest successes may seem at first to be those courses of action which are the biggest failures or the biggest affronts to happiness.

A graduate school at a well-known southern university decided to test its entering students on their knowledge of philosophy. Following the test, each student was required to take a course in philosophy.

At the end of the semester officials of the school were surprised to find their entrance test wasn't a very good measure of ultimate "success."

For example, the student who made the highest grade on the entrance exam did only a little better than average work in the class. The student with the second highest grade on the exam became discouraged in the middle of the semester and left school.

On the other hand, one student who had scored low on the entrance test became interested in what he was doing and finished up the semester with an "A" in philosophy.

What do we mean by success, anyway? Persons with the "biggest reputations" for popularity or brains don't always turn out that way. The real successes are not necessarily those with the reputations of being successful. In a deep sense the successful person may be one who works hard and quietly, and one who is interested in helping his fellows more than in promoting his own reputation.

The lasting victories are those that may be "invisible" at the moment. The world is filled with "successful" men and women who have never thought of anyone but themselves. Fortunately, there are also a few people around who define success not in terms of personal benefit, but in terms of the good they know they can accomplish—in the future, if not right now.

For a final definition of "success" the Christian turns to Christ for his pattern. We know him as a *failure* at getting favorable publicity or at avoiding hardship. We see him through the eyes of Isaiah, who described the coming Savior as a man

despised and rejected by men;
   a man of sorrows, and acquainted with grief
                    —Isa. 53:3

At the same time we know Christ as a *success* at bringing men to themselves and back into God's fellowship. Again, with Isaiah, we see him as one who has "borne our griefs and carried our sorrows."

But he was wounded for our transgression,
   he was bruised for our iniquities;
upon him was the chastisement that made us whole,
   and with his stripes we are healed.
All we like sheep have gone astray;
   we have turned every one to his own way;
and the Lord has laid on him the iniquity of us all.
                    —Isa. 53:5-6.

We know that as his followers we shall be required to follow him in hardship as well as joy, for "a servant is not greater than his master," and the trials of the master must fall upon the students (John 15:20). Yet we know that in him the victory over evil, sin, and suffering is certain.

Summary

At the beginning of this book, we decided that the subject of evil can't be fully understood just on the basis of talk, reading, or discussion. Yet, just as people like to talk about their operations, so they like to talk about their brushes with evil. Indeed, thoughtful people will benefit greatly from a discussion of this subject.

Though we cannot hope to remove all mystery from the suffering which all men undergo, perhaps we can honestly say we have discovered some helpful truths:

1. Evil is of two kinds—*physical* (floods, disease, accidents, death, and so on) and *moral* (all kinds of sin). Both kinds are real and cannot be explained away as imaginary or temporary.

2. The first kind, physical evil, is a genuine part of God's creation. By pitting their brains and strength against nature, men may have to suffer, yet this battle with physical evil tests our courage and is the basis of all progress.

3. We cannot explain physical evil as the result of God's wrath for our sins. Though we are sinful, God offers us his fellowship still. We know that God, in his Providence, has made the world as it is for a good purpose.

4. On the other hand, men create *moral* evil for themselves by their deliberate rebellion against God in selfishness, pride, and fear. One result of moral evil is immensely to complicate the suffering which men have to experience.

5. For all these reasons, then, suffering is an inescapable part of reality. We cannot avoid it, though with God's help we can fight it—opposing physical evil with our brains and other talents, and opposing moral evil with our resolve to turn toward God.

6. The Christian does not deliberately seek to suffer yet he knows full well that in his fight against evil, he must be prepared to suffer. In Christ he sees one who made the ultimate sacrifice—his own life—and like Christ, we must accept, wherever necessary, our share of suffering.

7. There is good evidence that we do not know life well until we have encountered its basic difficulties: the threat of death, the uncertainties of chance, the menace of pain, the burning fire of guilt, the shock of conflict when our beliefs meet opposition.

8. Back of these forms of suffering, however, we know that evil has been defeated once and for all in the victory of Christ over death. We are prepared to follow him in the knowledge that God's purpose will prevail.

WHAT DO YOU THINK?

1. If Christ has won a final victory over death, why should its benefits be delayed? Why do we, as men, have to experience death?

2. Describe someone whom you believe to be genuinely successful. What are the leading features of his character? What makes him, in your opinion, an authentic success?

3. How widespread is the following philosophy: "I do good only if it does me no harm or does not cost me too much." What is your honest opinion of it?

4. A scholar recently declared of the American people: "By and large, we do not want to know what, if anything, may lie beyond the grave. . . . We want, rather, the reassurance that we can and even now do count for something." What is your reaction? Can Christians share in any or all of this view?

5. Can one be a Christian without having heard of Christ?

6. Throughout Christian history there have been two schools of thought on the meaning of God's help: (1) It is something like a tool or crutch, which makes it easier for us to do what we can do anyway; (2) it is like breath, or an internal motor,

without which we could do nothing and would perish. Why has the church usually decided in favor of the second of these views?

7. What does John mean in his contrast between "light" and "darkness" (John 3:21)?

X

When You Face Suffering

IF WE COULD TRACE OUT OUR LIVES BY DRAWING A MAP of them, every conflict, emergency, and tragedy along the way would show up as a fork in the road. For most of us the rude shocks of life bring on one of two possible reactions. Either we accept them by a show of courage, or we stand frozen before them in despair.

Our reaction is hardly ever neutral or normal. When misfortune strikes, either we tend to rise above our usual performance or to fall below it.

In Graceville, Florida, the town shoemaker's house burst into flames one night. Awakened by the blaze, a man and his wife who live across the street rushed into the yard of the burning house and tried to awaken the occupants. Getting no response, they plunged inside and hastily searched every room.

They found no one there.

After leaving the fiercely burning house, the neighbor

couple realized they had burned themselves painfully. Courage had kept them going through their dangerous venture into the fire. Later, they learned, the shoemaker and his family had been out of the city.

Almost everyone knows of similar experiences. Frail women have shouldered invalids heavier than themselves to drag them from the flames. Men have braved gasoline fires to save fellow workers.

Almost everyone knows, too, of fires where the opposite reaction has set in—where not courage, but panic, has taken over.

One such tragedy occurred at Christmas, 1924, in Hobart, Oklahoma. A large crowd had assembled in a rural schoolhouse for the annual Christmas party. Flame from a candle touched off dry Christmas tree foliage, and the building quickly blazed out of control.

Those inside rushed for the door, but terror had replaced common sense. The door opened inward, and the frantic pressure of the crowd on it kept it tightly closed.

Thirty-seven people died. At the same time a three-year-old girl disappeared, and no one since has found what became of her. In one of the few courageous acts of that tragic evening the little girl's aunt—one of those to die—handed her out a window. But later, no one was able to find what became of her, and she is still missing.

The Crossroads in Every Life

We face the same crossroads—courageous advance or terrified retreat—every time personal misfortune threatens. Friends of a mild-mannered, studious senior theological student were surprised to find him serving as an usher at Vanderbilt University's Cole Lectures, for they knew his wife lay critically ill in the university hospital.

As the student reasoned it, his wife was too ill to have visitors, including himself. His only alternatives, then, were to retire to his apartment and wait or to go on with his life. That is why he stuck to his previous commitment and showed up at the auditorium to help seat the crowd.

His wife died only weeks before her husband was to graduate. Visibly shaken, he missed a few classes, but then he was back in his usual seat, looking older and a bit worn —but ready to face existence. He was graduated in the top fifth of his class.

"I considered dropping out of school," he admitted later, reflecting on the long ordeal he and his wife had shared. "But that would have made matters worse, not better."

How does one know whether he will react *this* way in a tragedy, with courage that pilots him through grief, or in the opposite way? There is no sure way of telling. It would be foolish to suggest some easy rule-of-thumb for making a prediction.

Yet one thing is certain according to Christian faith. You do not have to be able to manufacture courage all by yourself. There are two other resources—your neighbors and God. You can count on both. Of course, they cannot do your suffering for you, but they can share your burden and offer you their strength.

Our neighbors come to the rescue in one way, and God comes in another, more complete way. Let us look at both.

What Neighbors Are For

One spring night in 1957 more than 150 men gathered in the back yard of a house in Manorville, New York. Some of them hardly knew each other, and not all could claim to be friends of the people who lived in the house. Yet they had come together there in the most profound form of fellowship: a community effort to save a life.

Just before dark seven-year-old Benny Hooper had tumbled down a freshly dug twenty-one-foot wellshaft in the garden.

He had landed feet first with only one free hand above him—a hand he had vainly stretched upward with the pitiful cry, "Daddy." His father was unable to help him, and so the men of the community piled into the yard by the dozens.

All night long the determined men dug in shifts, slowly extending a rescue tunnel toward the bottom of the wellshaft. All the next day they dug.

Despair—always the great enemy when human beings have to deal with suffering—inevitably made its bid. "This is a lost cause," a deputy sheriff cried the next afternoon, but courage was there too, and the men kept digging, even though Benny now was silent and still and might well be dead.

Nearly twenty-four hours after Benny had fallen in the well, a small-framed construction worker wriggled into the well from the rescue shaft. As he pulled Benny out of the sand, the boy groaned. A few minutes later, when Benny and his rescuer were hauled out of the ground, a loud cheer went up.

The men of Manorville had saved Benny Hooper's life. They had come through with both physical power and inner courage during that long struggle with the imprisoning earth, and a battle against suffering had been won.

Fellowship is more profound when it is based on tragedy or misfortune than when it is based on the ordinary realities which bring men together—social acquaintance, business, geographical closeness. Moreover, the help men give one another in emergencies often goes beyond what they are likely to give on normal occasions. Suffering, then, can weld men together.

The Christian sees the basis for fellowship of every kind in the second great commandment: "You shall love your neighbor as yourself" (Mark 12:31). Benny Hooper's rescue is a powerful illustration of this commandment in practice. We are surely tempted to say that our chances of fulfilling it are better in the midst of tribulation than they are when the situation is normal, and no one gives others a second thought.

To see fully the role of the neighbor in suffering, we must notice one other point: neighborliness works both ways. We may not only *expect* help—both spiritual and physical—from others when we suffer; we must also *give* it. Indeed, that is one of the classical methods among Christians of treating their own misfortunes—by ministering to the misfortunes of others.

Perhaps you have been thinking, as you read this, that Benny Hooper's rescue was a rarity, the kind of exceptional event that would never happen to you. Here we must make a blunt suggestion. If no one seems to be rushing to your rescue, perhaps it is your own fault. For one becomes a neighbor basically by *being* a neighbor, by helping before being helped. After all, if everyone waited passively, there would be no communication between men at all. Besides, taking an interest in others will probably bleach your own troubles out by several shades. For the worst suffering of all, as Zossima reminds us in *The Brothers Karamazov*, is not being able to love others.

What Faith Can—and Cannot—Do

Jesus is careful to label the commandment about loving our neighbors as "Commandment Number Two." The *first* is to love God.

In the same way, we can say: When you face suffering, your neighbor is at best "Helper Number Two." Your first and greatest helper is God. Indeed, whatever help your neighbor can bring you, Christian faith holds, comes ultimately from God.

If we can put the notions of "courage" and "assistance" into quantitative terms for a moment, we can clarify the relation between God and neighbor. God is the originator of all courage and love; neighbors are the "wholesalers" or "distributors" of it. Whatever the degree of love we see being exchanged among neighbors, the Christian believes, God loves us even more, because he is the source of all love.

God's help to us, by that reasoning, should be even more spectacular than the kind of help rendered to Benny Hooper by the citizens of Manorville, New York, for God is the source, and men are the receivers of fellowship.

124

God's help *is* spectacular—it consists of everything that men do for each other as neighbors *plus* everything we receive from him directly as individuals—life, freedom, energy, courage, and patience.

God helps us through our neighbors by means of the fellowship we enjoy with them. He helps us as individuals chiefly by means of prayer.

"Every serious prayer contains power," says Paul Tillich, one of America's foremost theologians, "not because of the intensity of desire expressed in it, but because of the faith the person has in God's directing activity." Such faith, Tillich adds, can literally transform your situation by turning despair into courage.

Tillich does not mean that prayer is a magical gadget which can short-circuit the problems of life or insulate us from the rough and tumble of the world. It is rather a way of receiving God's help for *facing* the world and its problems.

When God comes to the rescue of a sufferer, let us note, he does not necessarily do so by removing the suffering. Sometimes, it is true, he does give *us* the means of removing the suffering. Medical science is one of the means he has given us. Accordingly, good health is more than a matter of prayer, or even of faith; it is a matter of taking advantage of the abilities which God has bestowed on men.

According to Karl Stern, a distinguished psychiatrist, it is a mistake to think that neurotic, worried people can always effect a cure on themselves simply by embracing religious faith. Religion must not be used as a "mental Band-aid," he warns. Rather, we must say, faith is to be

125

combined with the many talents God has given men, such as medical care.

Let us summarize what we have said about God's help to sufferers.

First, God offers us direct help through prayer. When we turn to him inwardly, we receive courage and hope, and even energy.

Second, God expects us to use the other means of help he has given us. These include the talents and gifts of neighbors—of all other men around us, such as the assistance of medical men.

When all this is said and done, however, one hard fact remains: we may have to suffer just the same. Prayer does not guarantee to relieve us of problems—it can give us, at most, a new outlook, a new spirit, renewed courage. The assistance of others, too, is not guaranteed to be perfect. Though medical science, for example, can cure some diseases, it is helpless before others. So there always is a residue of suffering which each of us has to undergo.

A Final Word

As we have already seen, in past chapters, suffering is part and parcel of the challenge of becoming God's followers. Without problems to solve and pain to endure and difficulties to overcome it is doubtful if there would be any progress or any civilization—or any full realization of our potential as men.

To this, we can add now only one thing. And that is the counsel of Jesus to all sufferers. "Blessed are those who mourn," he told the people who had come to hear him on the Mount, "for they shall be comforted" (Matt. 5:4).

Somehow, sooner or later, the suffering of the person of faith will be erased. Mourning will end in comfort, darkness will end in light. "You will be sorrowful," as Jesus said on another occasion, "but your sorrow will turn into joy" (John 16:20). The evils of this world, says Jesus, are like the pains of childbirth: When a woman is delivered of her child, "she no longer remembers the anguish, for joy that a child is born" (John 16:21).

In the end, we simply cannot find a ready explanation for *all* of the suffering and risk and hardship which life demands. We can only take Jesus' word for it: "So you have sorrow now, but I will see you again and your hearts will rejoice, and no one will take your joy from you" (John 16:22).

WHAT DO YOU THINK?

1. What changes are we expected to make in our lives as a result of the biblical commandment, "You shall love your neighbor as yourself"?

2. Why is good health more than a matter of faith healing?

3. Make a list of the opportunities you have passed up in the last few days to be a good neighbor by helping someone.

4. What results may we expect from prayer? What changes may prayer make in one's life? Are there some things we should not pray for?

5. Why is trouble often a firmer basis for fellowship than ordinary social relations? Should it be this way?

6. Here is a plea we often hear: "I'm no good at consoling people who have had a death in the family. I don't know what to say. Furthermore, I'm not much help at cheering up the

sick." What is your advice to a person like this? Should he visit anyway? Should he find other ways of expressing his concern?

7. Why is the most potent remedy for suffering—unselfish love of others—the one least often tried?